NP
NEWTON
PAGE

NEWTON PAGE

MATTHEW HOPKINS

WITCHFINDER GENERAL:

AN ANTHOLOGY

by

King James VI of Scotland, John Gaule & Matthew Hopkins

Selected and Edited

by

Eli Clarke

NEWTON PAGE

NEWTON PAGE

www.newtonpage.com

Matthew Hopkins
Witchfinder General:
An Anthology

Daemonologie (1597)
by King James VI of Scotland

The Witchcraft Act (1604)

Select Cases of Conscience Touching Witches and Witchcrafts (1646)
by John Gaule

The Discovery of Witches (1647)
by Matthew Hopkins

Selected and Edited by Eli Clarke

Published by Newton Page 2021

1 3 5 7 9 10 8 6 4 2

ISBN 978-1-934619-24-7

Printed in the United States of America
Set in Adobe Garamond Pro

CONTENTS

NOTE ON THE TEXT

Since each of the books and pamphlets contained in this collection were first published in the late sixteenth to mid-seventeenth-centuries, conventions of spelling, grammar, punctuation, expression, vocabulary and general notation have each undergone considerable modernization. In addition, the relatively crude practices of book and pamphlet production have been gradually replaced by the radically more exacting standards of modern publishing, which demand both uniformity of typesetting and editorial consistency. As a consequence of those changes, the modern reader is used to a more polished product than those available in the past.

However, notwithstanding the usual expectations of the modern reader, and in full appreciation that the original texts are not as easy on the modern eye as they would have been on their contemporary equivalents, the temptation to edit them to conform with modern writing and publishing conventions has been resisted. That approach has been taken because to do anything other than retain the original form of the texts would be to detract from their colorful character. The only minor exceptions to that approach have been the correction of dischordant italics and the replacement of the medial s with the modern s and the replacement of greek words with their English translations.

Each of the items were written for the consideration of the inhabitants of Great Britain. As such, each is tailored to conform with the conventional seventeenth-century stylistic expectations of a British readership. American readers will notice that in maintaining the integrity of the original publications, the original historic British forms of spelling have been retained. More generally, readers will notice both inconsistent and imaginative forms of spelling throughout.

Reproduced in this collection are the first editions and printings of:

Daemonologie (1597)
by King James VI of Scotland

The Witchcraft Act (1604)

Select Cases of Conscience Touching Witches and Witchcrafts (1646)
by John Gaule

Discovery of Witches (1647)
by Matthew Hopkins

DAEMONOLOGIE, IN FORME of a Dialogue,

Diuided into three Bookes.

EDINBVRGH

Printed by Robert Walde-graue

Printer to the Kings Majestie. An. 1597.

Cum Privilegio Regio.

DAEMONOLOGIE

IN FORME OF A DIALOGIE

DIUIDED INTO THREE BOOKES.

BY JAMES RX

PRINTED BY ROBERT WALDE-GRAUE,

PRINTER TO THE KINGS MAJESTIE. AN. 1597.

CUM PRIVILEGIO REGIO.

(1597)

THE PREFACE

THE PREFACE

TO THE READER

The fearefull aboundinge at this time in this countrie, of these detestable slaves of the Devill, the Witches or enchaunters, hath moved me (beloved reader) to dispatch in post, this following treatise of mine, not in any wise (as I protest) to serve for a shew of my learning & ingine, but onely (mooved of conscience) to preasse thereby, so farre as I can, to resolve the doubting harts of many; both that such assaultes of Sathan are most certainly practized, & that the instrumentes thereof, merits most severly to be punished: against the damnable opinions of two principally in our age, wherof the one called SCOT an Englishman, is not ashamed in publike print to deny, that ther can be such a thing as Witch-craft: and so mainteines the old error of the Sadducees, in denying of spirits. The other called WIERVS, a German Phisition, sets out a publick apologie for al these craftes-folkes, whereby, procuring for their impunitie, he plainely betrayes himselfe to have bene one of that profession.

And for to make this treatise the more pleasaunt and facill, I have put it in forme of a Dialogue, which I have divided into three bookes: The first speaking of Magic in general, and Necromancie in special. The second of Sorcerie and Witchcraft: and the thirde, conteines a discourse of all these kindes of spirits, & Spectres that appeares & trobles persones: together with a conclusion of the whol work.

My intention in this labour, is only to prove two things, as I have alreadie said: the one, that such divelish artes have bene and are. The other, what exact trial and severe punishment they merite: & therefore reason I, what kinde of things are possible to be performed in these arts, & by what naturall causes they may be, not that I touch every particular thing of the Devils power, for that were infinite: but onelie, to speak scholasticklie, (since this can not bee spoken in our language) I reason upon genus leaving species, and differentia to be comprehended therein.

As for example, speaking of the power of Magiciens, in the first book & sixt Chapter: I say, that they can suddenly cause be brought unto them, all kindes of daintie disshes, by their familiar spirit: Since as a thiefe he delightes to steale, and as a spirite, he can subtillie & suddenlie inough transport the same. Now under this genus may be comprehended al particulars, depending thereupon; Such as the bringing Wine out of a Wall, (as we have heard oft to have bene practised) and such others; which particulars, are sufficientlie proved by the reasons of the general. And such like in the second booke of Witch-craft in speciall, and fift Chap. I say and prove by diverse arguments, that Witches can, by the power of their Master, cure or cast on disseases: Now by these same reasones, that proves their power by the Devil of disseases in generally is aswell proved their power in speciall: as of weakening the nature of some men, to make them unable for women: and making it to abound in others, more then the ordinary course of nature would permit. And such like in all other particular sicknesses; But one thing I will pray thee to observe in all these places, where I reason upon the devils power, which is the different ends & scopes, that God as the first cause, and the Devill as his instrument and second cause shootes at in all these actiones of the Devil, (as Gods hang-man:) For where the devilles intention in them is ever to perish, either the soule or the body, or both of them, that he is so permitted to deale with: God by the contrarie, drawes ever out of that evill glorie to himselfe, either by the wracke of the wicked in his justice, or by the tryall of the patient, and amendment of the faithfull, being wakened up with that rod of correction.

Having thus declared unto thee then, my full intention in this Treatise, thou wilt easelie excuse, I doubt not, aswel my pretermitting, to declare the whole particular rites and secretes of these unlawfull artes: as also their infinite and wounderfull practises, as being neither of them pertinent to my purpose: the reason whereof, is given in the hinder ende of the first Chapter of the thirde booke: and who likes to be curious in these thinges, he may reade, if he will here of their practises, BODINUS Dæmonomanie, collected with greater diligence, then written with judgement, together with their confessions, that have bene at this time apprehened. If he would know what hath bene the opinion of the Auncientes, concerning their power: he shall see it wel described by HYPERIUS, & HEMMINGIUE, two late Germaine writers: Besides innumerable other neoterick Theologues, that writes largelie upon that subject: And if he woulde knowe what are the particuler rites, & curiosities of these black arts (which is both unnecessarie and perilous,) he will finde it in the fourth book of CORNELIUS Agrippa, and in VIERUS, whomof I spak.

And so wishing my pains in this Treatise (beloved Reader) to be effectual, in arming al them that reades the same, against these aboue mentioned erroures, and recommending my good will to thy friendly acceptation, I bid thee hartely fare-well.

JAMES Rx.

FIRST BOOKE

ARGUMENT

THE EXORD OF THE WHOLE. THE DESCRIPTION OF MAGIC IN SPECIALL.

CHAP. I.

ARGUMENT.

Proven by the Scripture, that these unlawfull artes in genere, have bene and may be put in practise.

Philomathes and Epistemon reason the matter.

Philomathes. I am surely verie glad to have mette with you this daye, for I am of opinion, that ye can better resolve me of some thing, wherof I stand in great doubt, nor anie other whom-with I could have mette.

Epi. In what I can, that ye like to speir at me, I will willinglie and freelie tell my opinion, and if I prove it not sufficiently, I am heartely content that a better reason carie it away then.

Phi. What thinke yee of these strange newes, which now onelie furnishes purpose to al men at their meeting: I meane of these Witches?

Epi. Surelie they are wonderfull: And I think so cleare and

plaine confessions in that purpose, have never fallen out in anie age or cuntrey.

Phi. No question if they be true, but thereof the Doctours doubtes.

Epi. What part of it doubt ye of?

Phi. Even of all, for ought I can yet perceaue: and namelie, that there is such a thing as Witch-craft or Witches, and I would pray you to resolve me thereof if ye may: for I have reasoned with sundrie in that matter, and yet could never be satisfied therein.

Epi. I shall with good will doe the best I can: But I thinke it the difficiller, since ye denie the thing it selfe in generall: for as it is said in the logick schools, Contra negantem principia non est disputandum. Alwaies for that part, that witchcraft, and Witches have bene, and are, the former part is clearelie proved by the Scriptures, and the last by dailie experience and confessions.

Phi. I know yee will alleadge me Saules Pythonisse: but that as appeares will not make much for you.

Epi. Not onlie that place, but divers others: But I marvel why that should not make much for me?

Phi. The reasones are these, first yee may consider, that Saul being troubled in spirit, and having fasted long before, as the text testifieth,[1] and being come to a woman that was bruted to have such knowledge, and that to inquire so important news,

1. 1. Sam. 28.

he having so guiltie a conscience for his hainous offences, and specially, for that same unlawful curiositie, and horrible defection: and then the woman crying out upon the suddaine in great admiration, for the uncouth sicht that she alledged to have sene, discovering him to be the King, thogh disguysed, & denied by him before: it was no wounder I say, that his senses being thus distracted, he could not perceave hir faining of hir voice, hee being himselfe in an other chalmer, and seeing nothing. Next what could be, or was raised? The spirit of Samuel? Prophane and against all Theologie: the Divell in his likenes? as unappeirant, that either God would permit him to come in the shape of his Saintes (for then could never the Prophets in those daies have bene sure, what Spirit spake to them in their visiones) or then that he could fore-tell what was to come there after; for Prophecie proceedeth onelie of GOD: and the Devill hath no knowledge of things to come.

Epi. Yet if yee will marke the wordes of the text, ye will finde clearely, that Saul saw that apparition: for giving you that Saul was in an other Chalmer, at the making of the circles & conjurationes, needeful for that purpose (as none of that craft will permit any others to behold at that time) yet it is evident by the text, that how sone that once that unclean spirit was fully risen, shee called in upon Saul. For it is saide in the text, that Saule knew him to be Samuel, which coulde not have bene, by the hearing tell onely of an olde man with an mantil, since there was many mo old men dead in Israel nor Samuel: And the common weid of that whole Cuntrey was mantils. As to the next, that it was not the spirit of Samuel, I grant: In the proving whereof ye neede not to insist, since all Christians of whatso-ever Religion agrees upon that: and none but either mere ignorants, or Necromanciers or Witches doubtes thereof. And that the Divel is permitted at som-times to put himself in the liknes of the Saintes, it is plaine in the Scriptures, where it is said, that Sathan can trans-forme himselfe into an Angell of light.[2] Neither could that bring any inconvenient with the visiones of the Prophets, since it is most certaine, that God will not permit him so to deceive his own: but only such, as first wilfully deceives them-selves, by running unto him, whome God then suffers to fall in their owne snares, and justlie permittes them to be illuded with great efficacy of deceit, because they would not beleeve the trueth (as Paul sayth). And as to the divelles foretelling of things to come, it is true that he knowes not all things future, but yet that he knowes parte, the Tragicall event of this historie declares it, (which the wit of woman could never have fore-spoken) not that he hath any prescience, which is only proper to God: or yet knows anie thing by loking upon God, as in a mirrour (as the good Angels doe) he being for ever debarred from the favorable presence & countenance of his creator, but only by one of these two meanes, either as being worldlie wise, and taught by an continuall experience, ever since the creation, judges by likelie-hood of thinges to come, according to the like that hath passed before, and the naturall causes, in respect of the vicissitude of all thinges worldly: Or else by Gods employing of him in a turne, and so foreseene thereof: as appeares to have bin in this, whereof we finde the verie like in Micheas propheticque discourse to King Achab.[3] But to proove this my first proposition, that there can be such a thing as witch-craft, & witches, there are manie mo places in the Scriptures then this (as I said before). As first in the law of God, it is plainely prohibited:[4] But certaine it is, that the Law of God speakes nothing in vaine, nether doth it lay curses, or injoyne punishmentes upon shaddowes, condemning that to

2. 2. Cor. 11.14.

3. 1. King. 22.

4. Exod. 22.

be il, which is not in essence or being as we call it. Secondlie it is plaine, where wicked Pharaohs wise-men imitated ane number of Moses miracles, to harden the tyrants heart there by.[5] Thirdly, said not Samuell to Saull, that disobedience is as the sinne of Witch-craft? [6] To compare to a thing that were not, it were too too absurd. Fourthlie, was not Simon Magus, a man of that craft? And fiftlie, what was she that had the spirit of Python? [7] beside innumerable other places that were irkesom to recite.[8]

5. Exod. 7 & 8.

6. 1. Sam. 15.

7. Acts. 8.

8. Acts 16.

CHAP. II.

ARGUMENT.

What kynde of sin the practizers of these unlawfull artes committes. The division of these artes. And what are the meanes that allures any to practize them.

Philomathes. But I thinke it very strange, that God should permit anie man-kynde (since they beare his owne Image) to fall in so grosse and filthie a defection.

Epi. Although man in his Creation was made to the Image of the Creator,[1] yet through his fall having once lost it, it is but restored againe in a part by grace onelie to the elect: So all the rest falling away from God, are given over in the handes of the Devill that enemie, to beare his Image: and being once so given over, the greatest and the grossest impietie, is the pleasantest, and most delytefull unto them.

Phi. But may it not suffice him to have indirectly the rule, and procure the perdition of so manie soules by alluring them to vices, and to the following of their own appetites, suppose

1. Gen. 1.

he abuse not so many simple soules, in making them directlie acknowledge him for their maister.

Epi. No surelie, for hee uses everie man, whom of he hath the rule, according to their complexion and knowledge: And so whome he findes most simple, he plaineliest discovers himselfe unto them. For hee beeing the enemie of mans Salvation, uses al the meanes he can to entrappe them so farre in his snares, as it may be unable to them thereafter (suppose they would) to rid themselves out of the same.

Phi. Then this sinne is a sinne against the holie Ghost.

Epi. It is in some, but not in all.

Phi. How that? Are not all these that runnes directlie to the Devill in one Categorie.

Epi. God forbid, for the sin against the holie Ghost hath two branches: The one a falling backe from the whole service of GOD, and a refusall of all his preceptes. The other is the doing of the first with knowledge, knowing that they doe wrong against their own conscience, and the testimonie of the holie Spirit, having once had a tast of the sweetnes of Gods mercies.[2] Now in the first of these two, all sortes of Necromancers, Enchanters or Witches, ar comprehended: but in the last, none but such as erres with this knowledge that I have spoken of.

Phi. Then it appeares that there are more sortes nor one, that are directlie professors of his service: and if so be, I pray you tell me how manie, and what are they?

2. Heb. 6. 10.

Epi. There are principallie two sortes, whereunto all the partes of that unhappie arte are redacted; whereof the one is called Magic or Necromancie, the other Sorcerie or Witch-craft.

Phi. What I pray you? and how manie are the meanes, whereby the Devill allures persones in anie of these snares?

Epi. Even by these three passiones that are within our selves: Curiositie in great ingines: thrist of revenge, for some tortes deeply apprehended: or greedie appetite of geare, caused through great poverty. As to the first of these, Curiosity, it is onelie the inticement of Magiciens, or Necromanciers: and the other two are the allureres of the Sorcerers, or Witches, for that olde and craftie Serpent, being a spirite, hee easilie spyes our affections, and so conformes himselfe thereto, to deceave us to our wracke.

CHAP. III.

ARGUMENT.

The significations and Etymologies of the words of Magic and Necromancie. The difference betuixt Necromancie and Witchcraft: What are the entressis, and beginninges, that brings anie to the knowledge thereof.

Philomathes. I Would gladlie first heare, what thing is it that ye call Magic or Necromancie.

Epi. This worde Magic in the Persian toung, importes as muche as to be ane contemplator or Interpretour of Divine and heavenlie sciences: which being first used amongs the Chaldees, through their ignorance of the true divinitie, was esteemed and reputed amongst them, as a principall vertue: And therefore, was named unjustlie with an honorable stile, which name the Greekes imitated, generally importing all these kindes of unlawfull artes. And this word Necromancie is a Greek word, compounded of (nekron) and (manteia), which is to say, the Prophecie by the dead. This last name is given, to this black & unlawfull science by the figure Synedoche, because it is a principal part of that art, to serue them selves with dead carcages in their divinations.

Phi. What difference is there betwixt this arte, and Witch-craft.

Epi. Surelie, the difference vulgare put betwixt them, is verrie merrie, and in a maner true; for they say, that the Witches ar servantes onelie, and slaves to the Devil; but the Necromanciers are his maisters and commanders.

Phi. How can that be true, yt any men being specially adicted to his service, can be his commanders?

Epi. Yea, they may be: but it is onelie secundum quid: For it is not by anie power that they can have over him, but ex pacto allanerlie: whereby he oblices himself in some trifles to them, that he may on the other part obteine the fruition of their body & soule, which is the onlie thing he huntes for.

Phi. An verie in-æquitable contract forsooth: But I pray you discourse unto mee, what is the effect and secreets of that arte?

Epi. That is over large an fielde ye give mee: yet I shall doe good-will, the most summarlie that I can, to runne through the principal points thereof. As there are two sorts of folkes, that may be entysed to this arte, to wit, learned or unlearned: so is there two meanes, which are the first steerers up & feeders of their curiositie, thereby to make them to give themselves over to the same: Which two meanes, I call the Divels schoole, and his rudimentes. The learned have their curiositie wakened uppe; and fedde by that which I call his schoole: this is the Astrologie judiciar. For divers men having attained to a great perfection in learning, & yet remaining overbare (alas) of the spirit of regeneration and frutes thereof: finding all naturall thinges common, aswell to the stupide pedants as unto them, they assaie to vendicate unto them a greater name, by not onlie knowing the course of things heavenlie, but likewise to cling to the knowledge of things to come thereby. Which, at the first face appearing lawfull unto them, in respect the ground therof seemeth to proceed of naturall causes onelie: they are so allured thereby, that finding their practize to proove true in sundry things, they studie to know the cause thereof: and so mounting from degree to degree, upon the slipperie and uncertaine scale of curiositie; they are at last entised, that where lawfull artes or sciences failes, to satisfie their restles mindes, even to seeke to that black and unlawfull science of Magie. Where, finding at the first, that such divers formes of circles & conjurations rightlie joyned thereunto, will raise such divers formes of spirites, to resolve them of their doubts: and attributing the doing thereof, to the power inseparablie tyed, or inherent in the circles: and manie words of God, confusedlie wrapped in; they blindlie glorie of themselves, as if they had by their quicknes of ingine, made a conquest of Plutoes dominion, and were become Emperours over the Stygian habitacles. Where, in the meane time (miserable wretches) they are become in verie deede, bond-slaves to their mortall enemie: and their knowledge, for all that they presume thereof, is nothing increased, except in knowing evill, and the horrors of Hell for punishment thereof, as Adams was by the eating of the forbidden tree.[1]

1. Gen. 3.

CHAP. IV.

ARGUMENT.

The Description of the Rudiments and Schoole, which are the entresses to the arte of Magie: And in speciall the differences betwixt Astronomie and Astrologie: Division of Astrologie in divers partes.

Philomathes. But I pray you likewise forget not to tell what are the Devilles rudimentes.

Epi. His rudimentes, I call first in generall, all that which is called vulgarly the vertue of worde, herbe, & stone: which is used by unlawful charmes, without naturall causes. As likewise all kinde of practicques, freites, or other like extraordinarie actiones, which cannot abide the true toutche of naturall reason.

Phi. I would have you to make that playner, by some particular examples; for your proposition is verie generall.

Epi. I meane either by such kinde of Charmes as commonlie dafte wives uses, for healing of forspoken goodes, for preseruing them from evill eyes, by knitting roun-trees, or sundriest kinde of herbes, to the haire or tailes of the goodes: By curing the Worme, by stemming of blood, by healing of Horse-crookes, by turning of the riddle, or doing of such like innumerable things by wordes, without applying anie thing, meete to the part offended, as Mediciners doe; Or else by staying maried folkes, to have naturallie adoe with other, (by knitting so manie knottes upon a poynt at the time of their mariage). And such-like things, which men uses to practise in their merrinesse: For fra unlearned men (being naturallie curious, and lacking the true knowledge of God) findes these practises to proove true, as sundrie of them will doe, by the power of the Devill for deceauing men, and not by anie inherent vertue in these vaine wordes and freites; & being desirous to winne a reputation to themselves in such-like turnes, they either (if they be of the shamefaster sorte) seeke to bee learned by some that are experimented in that Arte, (not knowing it to be evill at the first) or else being of the grosser sorte, runnes directlie to the Devill for ambition or desire of gaine, and plainelie contractes with him thereupon.

Phi. But me thinkes these meanes which yee call the Schoole and rudimentes of the Devill, are thinges lawfull, and have bene approoved for such in all times and ages: As in special, this science of Astrologie, which is one of the speciall members of the Mathematicques.

Epi. There are two thinges which the learned have observed from the beginning, in the science of the Heavenlie Creatures, the Planets, Starres, and such like: The one is their course and ordinary motiones, which for that cause is called Astronomia: Which word is a compound of (nomos) and (asteron) that is to say, the law of the Starres: And this arte indeed is one of the members of the Mathematicques, & not onelie lawful, but most necessarie and commendable. The other is called Astrologia, being compounded of (asteron) and (logos) which is to say, the word, and preaching of the starres: Which is deuided in two partes: The first by knowing thereby the powers of simples, and sickenesses, the course of the seasons and the weather, being ruled by their influence; which part depending upon the former, although it be not of it selfe a parte of Mathematicques: yet it is not unlawful, being moderatlie used, suppose not so necessarie and commendable as the former. The second part is to truste so much to their influences, as thereby to fore-tell what common-weales shall florish or decay: what persones shall be fortunate or unfortunate: what side shall winne in anie battell: What man shall obteine victorie at singular combate: What way, and of what age shall men die: What horse shall winne at matche-running; and diverse such like incredible things, wherein Cardanus, Cornelius Agrippa, and diverse others have more curiouslie then profitably written at large. Of this roote last spoken of, springs innumerable branches; such as the knowledge by the natiuities; the Cheiromancie, Geomantie, Hydromantie, Arithmantie, Physiognomie: & a thousand others: which were much practised, & holden in great reverence by the Gentles of olde. And this last part of Astrologie whereof I have spoken, which is the root of their branches, was called by them pars fortunæ. This parte now is utterlie unlawful to be trusted in, or practized amongst christians, as leaning to no ground of natural reason: & it is this part which I called before the devils schole.

Phi. But yet manie of the learned are of the contrarie opinion.

Epi. I grant, yet I could give my reasons to fortifie & maintaine my opinion, if to enter into this disputation it wold not draw me quite off the ground of our discours; besides the mis-spending of the whole daie thereupon: One word onely I will answet to them, & that in the Scriptures (which must be an infallible ground to all true Christians)[1] That in the Prophet Jeremie it is plainelie forbidden, to beleeve or hearken unto them that Prophecies & fore-speakes by the course of the Planets & Starres.

1. Jerem. 10.

CHAP. V.

ARGUMENT.

How farre the using of Charmes is lawfull or unlawfull: The description of the formes of Circkles and Coniurationes. And what causeth the Magicianes themselves to wearie thereof.

Philomathes. Wel, Ye have said far inough in that argument. But how proove ye now that these charmes or unnaturall practicques are unlawfull: For so, many honest & merrie men & women have publicklie practized some of them, that I thinke if ye would accuse them al of Witch-craft, ye would affirme more nor ye will be beleeved in.

Epi. I see if you had taken good tent (to the nature of that word, whereby I named it,) ye would not have bene in this doubt, nor mistaken me, so farre as ye have done: For although, as none can be schollers in a schole, & not be subject to the master thereof: so none can studie and put in practize (for studie the alone, and knowledge, is more perilous nor offensive; and it is the practise only that makes the greatnes of the offence.) the cirkles and art of Magie, without committing an horrible defection from God: And yet as they that reades and learnes their rudiments, are not the more subject to anie schoole-master, if it please not their parentes to put them to the schoole thereafter; So they who ignorantly proves these practicques, which I cal the devilles rudiments, unknowing them to be baites, casten out by him, for trapping such as God will permit to fall in his hands: This kinde of folkes I saie, no doubt, ar to be judged the best of, in respect they use no invocation nor help of him (by their knowledge at least) in these turnes, and so have never entred themselves in Sathans service; Yet to speake truely for my owne part (I speake but for my selfe) I desire not to make so neere riding: For in my opinion our enemie is over craftie, and we over weake (except the greater grace of God) to assay such hazards, wherein he preases to trap us.

Phi. Ye have reason forsooth; for as the common Proverbe saith: They that suppe keile with the Devill, have neede of long spoones. But now I praie you goe forwarde in the describing of this arte of Magie.

Epi. Fra they bee come once unto this perfection in evill, in having any knowledge (whether learned or unlearned) of this black art: they then beginne to be wearie of the raising of their Maister, by conjured circkles; being both so difficile and perilous, and so commeth plainelie to a contract with him, wherein is speciallie conteined formes and effectes.

Phi. But I praye you or ever you goe further, discourse me somewhat of their circkles and conjurationes; And what should be the cause of their wearying thereof: For it should seeme that that forme should be lesse fearefull yet, than the direct haunting and societie, with that foule and uncleane Spirite.

Epi. I thinke ye take me to be a Witch my selfe, or at the least would faine sweare your selfe prentise to that craft: Alwaies as I may, I shall shortlie satisfie you, in that kinde of conjurations, which are conteined in such bookes, which I call the Devilles Schoole: There are foure principall partes; the persons of the conjurers; the action of the conjuration; the wordes and rites used to that effect; and the Spirites that are conjured. Ye must first remember to laye the ground, that I tould you before: which is, that it is no power inherent in the circles, or in the holines of the names of God blasphemouslie used: nor in whatsoever rites or ceremonies at that time used, that either can raise any infernall spirit, or yet limitat him perforce within or without these circles. For it is he onelie, the father of all lyes, who having first of all prescribed that forme of doing, feining himselfe to be commanded & restreined thereby, wil be loath to passe the boundes of these injunctiones; aswell thereby to make them glory in the impiring over him (as I saide before:) As likewise to make himselfe so to be trusted in these little thinges, that he may have the better commoditie thereafter, to deceive them in the end with a tricke once for all; I meane the everlasting perdition of their soul & body. Then laying this ground, as I have said, these conjurationes must have few or mo in number of the persones conjurers (alwaies passing the singuler number) according to the qualitie of the circle, and forme of apparition. Two principall thinges cannot well in that errand be wanted: holie-water (whereby the Devill mockes the Papistes) and some present of a liuing thing unto him. There ar likewise certaine seasons, dayes and houres, that they observe in this purpose: These things being all readie, and prepared, circles are made triangular, quadrangular, round, double or single, according to the forme of apparition that they craue. But to speake of the diverse formes of the circles, of the innumerable characters and crosses that are within and without, and out-through the same, of the divers formes of apparitiones, that that craftie spirit illudes them with, and or all such particulars in that action, I remit it to over-manie that have busied their heades in describing of the same; as being but curious, and altogether unprofitable. And this farre onelie I touch, that when the conjured Spirit appeares, which will not be while after manie circumstances, long praiers, and much muttring and murmuring of the conjurers; like a Papist priest, dispatching a hunting Masse: how sone I say, he appeares, if they have missed one iote of all their rites; or if any of their feete once slyd over the circle through terror of his feareful apparition, he payes himselfe at that time in his owne hande, of that due debt which they ought him; and other-wise would have delayed longer to have payed him: I meane hee carries them with him bodie and soule. If this be not now a just cause to make them wearie of these formes of conjuration, I leave it to you to judge upon; considering the long-somenesse of the labour, the precise keeping of dayes and houres (as I have said), the terriblenesse of apparition, and the present perrell that they stande in, in missing the least circumstance or freite, that they ought to observe: And on the other parte, the Devil is glad to mooue them to a plaine and square dealing with him as I said before.

CHAP. VI.

ARGUMENT.

The Devilles contract with the Magicians: The division thereof in two partes: What is the difference betwixt Gods miracles and the Devils.

Philomathes. Indeede there is cause inough, but rather to leave him at all, then to runne more plainlie to him, if they were wise he delt with. But goe forwards now I pray you to these turnes, fra they become once deacons in this craft.

Epi. From time that they once plainelie begin to contract with him: The effect of their contract consistes in two thinges; in formes and effectes, as I began to tell alreadie, were it not yee interrupted me (for although the contract be mutuall; I speake first of that part, wherein the Devill oblishes himselfe to them) by formes, I meane in what shape or fashion he shall come unto them, when they call upon him. And by effectes, I understand, in what special sorts of services he bindes himselfe to be subject unto them. The qualitie of these formes and effectes, is lesse or greater, according to the skil and art of the Magician. For as to the formes, to some of the baser sorte of them he oblishes him selfe to appeare at their calling upon him, by such a proper name which he shewes unto them, either in likenes of a dog, a Catte, an Ape, or such-like other beast; or else to answere by a voyce onlie. The effects are to answere to such demands, as concernes curing of disseases, their own particular menagery: or such other base things as they require of him. But to the most curious sorte, in the formes he will oblish himselfe, to enter in a dead bodie, and there out of to give such answers, of the event of battels, of maters concerning the estate of commonwelths, and such like other great questions: yea, to some he will be a continuall attender, in forme of a Page: He will permit himselfe to be conjured, for the space of so many yeres, ether in a tablet or a ring, or such like thing, which they may easely carrie about with them: He gives them power to sel such wares to others, whereof some will bee dearer, and some better cheape; according to the lying or true speaking of the Spirit that is conjured therein. Not but that in verie deede, all Devils must be lyars; but so they abuse the simplicitie of these wretches, that becomes their schollers, that they make them beleeve, that at the fall of Lucifer, some Spirites fell in the aire, some in the fire, some in the water, some in the lande: In which Elementes they still remaine. Whereupon they build, that such as fell in the fire, or in the aire, are truer then they, who fell in the water or in the land, which is al but meare trattles, & forged by the author of al deceit. For they fel not be weight, as a solide substance, to stick in any one parte: But the principall part of their fal, consisting in qualitie, by the falling from the grace of God wherein they were created, they continued still thereafter, and shal do while the latter daie, in wandring through the worlde, as Gods hang-men, to execute such turnes as he employes them in. And when anie of them are not occupyed in that, returne they must to their prison in hel (as it is plaine in the miracle that Christ wrought at Gennezareth)[1] therein at the latter daie to be all enclosed for ever: and as they deceive their schollers in this, so do they, in imprinting in them the opinion that there are so manie Princes, Dukes, and Kinges amongst them, everie one commanding fewer or mo Legions, and impyring in divers artes, and quarters of the earth. For though that I will not denie that there be a forme of ordour amongst the Angels in Heaven, and consequentlie, was amongst them before their fall; yet, either that they bruike the same sensine; or that God will permit us to know by damned Devils, such Heavenlie mysteries of his, which he would not reveale to us neither by Scripture nor Prophets, I thinke no Christiane will once thinke it. But by the contrarie of all such mysteries, as he hath closed up with his seale of secrecie; it becommeth us to be contented with an humble ignorance, they being thinges not necessarie for our saluation. But to returne to the purpose, as these formes, wherein Sathan oblishes himselfe to the greatest of the Magicians, are wounderfull curious; so are the effectes correspondent unto the same: For he will oblish himselfe to teach them artes and sciences, which he may easelie doe, being so learned a knaue as he is: To carrie them newes from anie parte of the worlde, which the agilitie of a Spirite may easelie performe: to reveale to them the secretes of anie persons, so being they bee once spoken, for the thought none knowes but GOD; except so far as yee may ghesse by their countenance, as one who is doubtleslie learned, inough in the Physiognomie: Yea, he will make his schollers to creepe in credite with Princes, by fore-telling them manie greate thinges; parte true, parte false: For if all were false, he would tyne credite at all handes; but alwaies doubtsome, as his Oracles were. And he will also make them to please Princes, by faire banquets and daintie dishes, carryed in short space fra the farthest part of the worlde. For no

1. Mat. 8.

man doubts but he is a thiefe, and his agilitie (as I spake before) makes him to come suche speede. Such-like, he will guard his schollers with faire armies of horse-men and foote-men in appearance, castles and fortes: Which all are but impressiones in the aire, easelie gathered by a spirite, drawing so neare to that substance himselfe: As in like maner he will learne them manie juglarie trickes at Gardes, dice, & such like, to deceive mennes senses thereby: and such innumerable false practicques; which are proven by over-manie in this age: As they who ar acquainted with that Italian called Scoto yet liuing, can reporte. And yet are all these thinges but deluding of the senses, and no waies true in substance, as were the false miracles wrought by King Pharaoes Magicians, for counterfeiting Moyses: For that is the difference betuixt Gods myracles and the Devils, God is a creator, what he makes appeare in miracle, it is so in effect. As Moyses rod being casten downe, was no doubt turned in a natural Serpent: where as the Devill (as Gods Ape) counterfetting that by his Magicians, maid their wandes to appeare so, onelie to mennes outward senses: as kythed in effect by their being deuoured by the other. For it is no wonder, that the Devill may delude our senses, since we see by common proofe, that simple juglars will make an hundreth thinges seeme both to our eies and eares otherwaies then they are. Now as to the Magicians parte of the contract, it is in a word that thing, which I said before, the Devill hunts for in all men.

Phi. Surelie ye have said much to me in this arte, if all that ye have said be as true as wounderfull.

Epi. For the trueth in these actiones, it will be easelie confirmed, to anie that pleases to take paine upon the reading of diverse authenticque histories, and the inquiring of daily experiences. And as for the trueth of their possibilitie, that they may be, and in what maner, I trust I have alleaged nothing whereunto I have not joyned such probable reasons, as I leave to your discretion, to waie and consider: One word onlie I omitted; concerning the forme of making of this contract, which is either written with the Magicians owne bloud: or else being agreed upon (in termes his schole-master) touches him in some parte, though peraduenture no marke remaine: as it doth with all Witches.

CHAP. VII.

ARGUMENT.

The reason why the art of Magic is unlawfull.
What punishment they merite:
And who may be accounted guiltie of that crime.

Philomathes. Surelie Ye have made this arte to appeare verie monstruous & detestable. But what I pray you shall be said to such as mainteines this art to be lawfull, for as evill as you have made it?

Epi. I say, they sauour of the panne them selues, or at least little better, And yet I would be glad to heare their reasons.

Phi. There are two principallie, that ever I heard used; beside that which is founded upon the common Proverb (that the Necromancers commands the Devill, which ye have already refuted). The one is grounded upon a received custome: The other upon an authoritie, which some thinkes infallible. Upon custome, we see that diverse Christian Princes and Magistrates severe punishers of Witches, will not onelie over-see Magicians to live within their dominions; but even some-times delight to see them proove some of their practicques. The other reason is, that Moyses being brought up (as it is expreslie said in the Scriptures) in all the sciences of the Ægyptians; whereof no doubt, this was one of the principalles. And he notwithstanding of this arte, pleasing God, as he did, consequentlie that art professed by so godlie a man, coulde not be unlawfull.

Epi. As to the first of your reasones, grounded upon custome: I saie, an evill custome can never be accepted for a good law, for the over great ignorance of the worde in some Princes and Magistrates, and the contempt thereof in others, moues them to sinne heavelie against their office in that poynt. As to the other reasone, which seemes to be of greater weight, if it were formed in a Syllogisme; it behooued to be in manie termes, and full of fallacies (to speake in termes of Logicque) for first, that that generall proposition; affirming Moyses to be taught in all the sciences of the Ægyptians, should conclude that he was taught in Magie, I see no necessity. For we must understand that the spirit of God there, speaking of sciences, understandes them that are lawfull; for except they be lawfull, they are but abusiuè called sciences, & are but ignorances indeede: Nam homo pictus, non est homo. Secondlie, giuing that he had bene taught in it, there is great difference, betwixt knowledge and practising of a thing (as I said before). For God knoweth all thinges, being alwaies good, and of our sinne & our infirmitie proceedeth our ignorance. Thirdlie, giuing that he had both studied and practised the same (which is more nor monstruous to be beleeved by any Christian) yet we know well inough, that before that ever the spirite of God began to call Moyses, he was fled out of Ægypt, being fourtie yeares of age, for the slaughter of anÆgyptian, and in his good-father Iethroes lande, first called at the firie bushe, having remained there other fourtie yeares in exile: so that suppose he had beene the wickeddest man in the worlde before, he then became a changed and regenerat man, and very litle of olde Moyses remained in him. Abraham was an Idolater in Ur of the Chaldeans, before he was called: And Paule being called Saule, was a most sharp persecutor of the Saintes of God, while that name was changed.

Phi. What punishment then thinke ye merites these Magicians and Necromancers?

Epi. The like no doubt, that Sorcerers and Witches merites; and rather so much greater, as their error proceedes of the greater knowledge, and so drawes nerer to the sin against the holy Ghost. And as I saye of them, so saye I the like of all such as consults, enquires, entertaines, & oversees them, which is seene by the miserable endes of many that askes councell of them: For the Devill hath never better tydings to tell to any, then he tolde to Saule: neither is it lawfull to use so unlawfull instrumentes, were it never for so good a purpose: for that axiome in Theologie is most certaine and infallible: Nunquam faciendum est malum ut bonum inde eueniat.[1]

1. Ast 3.

SECONDE BOOKE

ARGUMENT

THE DESCRIPTION OF SORCERIE AND WITCHCRAFT IN SPECIALL.

CHAP. I.

ARGUMENT.

Proved by the Scripture, that such a thing can be: And the reasones refuted of all such as would call it but an imagination and Melancholicque humor.

Philomathes. Now since yee have satisfied me nowe so fullie, concerning Magic or Necromancie I will pray you to do the like in Sorcerie or Witchcraft.

Epi. That fielde is likewise verie large: and althought in the mouthes and pennes of manie, yet fewe knowes the trueth thereof, so wel as they beleeve themselves, as I shall so shortely as I can, make you (God willing) as easelie to perceive.

Phi. But I pray you before ye goe further, let mee interrupt you here with a shorte digression: which is, that manie can scarcely beleeve that there is such a thing as Witch-craft. Whose reasons I wil shortely alleage unto you, that ye may satisfie me as well in that, as ye have done in the rest. For first, whereas the Scripture seemes to proove Witchcraft to be, by diverse examples, and speciallie by sundrie of the same, which ye have alleaged, it is thought by some, that these places speakes of Magicians and Necromancers onlie, & not of Witches. As in special, these wise men of Pharaohs, that counterfeited Moyses miracles, were Magicianssay they, & not Witches: As likewise that Pythonisse that Saul consulted with: And so was Simon Magus in the new Testament, as that very stile importes. Secondlie, where ye would oppone the dailie practicque, & confession of so manie, that is thought likewise to be but verie melancholicque imaginations of simple rauing creatures. Thirdly, if Witches had such power of Witching of folkes to death, (as they say they have) there had bene none left alive long sence in the world, but they: at the least, no good or godlie person of whatsoever estate, coulde have escaped their devilrie.

Epi. Your three reasons as I take, ar grounded the first of them negativè upon the Scripture: The second affirmativè upon Physicke: And the thirde upon the certaine proofe of experience. As to your first, it is most true indeede, that all these wise men of Pharaoh were Magicians of art: As likewise it appeares wel that the Pythonisse, with whom Saul consulted, was of that same profession: & so was Simon Magus. But yee omitted to speake of the Lawe of God, wherein are all Magicians, Divines, Enchanters, Sorcerers, Witches, & whatsover of that kinde that consultes with the Devill, plainelie prohibited, and alike threatned against. And besides that, she who had the Spirite of Python, in the Actes,[1] whose Spirite was put to silence by the Apostle, coulde be no other thing but a verie Sorcerer or Witch, if ye admit the vulgare distinction, to be in a maner true, whereof I spake in the beginning of our conference. For that spirit whereby she conquested such gaine to her Master, was not at her raising or commanding, as she pleased to appoynt, but spake by her toung, aswel publicklie, as privatelie: Whereby she

1. Act. 16.

seemed to draw nearer to the sort of Demoniakes or possessed, if that conjunction betwixt them, had not bene of her owne consent: as it appeared by her, not being tormented therewith: And by her conquesting of such gaine to her masters (as I have alreadie said.) As to your second reason grounded upon Physick, in attributing their confessiones or apprehensiones, to a naturall melancholicque humour: Anie that pleases Physicallie to consider upon the naturall humour of melancholie, according to all the Physicians, that ever writ thereupon, they shall finde that that will be over short a cloak to cover their knauery with: For as the humor of Melancholie in the selfe is blacke, heauie and terrene, so are the symptomes thereof, in any persones that are subject thereunto, leannes, palenes, desire of solitude: and if they come to the highest degree therof, mere folie and Manie: where as by the contrarie, a great nomber of them that ever have bene convict or confessors of Witchcraft, as may be presently seene by manie that have at this time confessed: they are by the contrarie, I say, some of them rich and worldly-wise, some of them fatte or corpulent in their bodies, and most part of them altogether given over to the pleasures of the flesh, continual haunting of companie, and all kind of merrines, both lawfull and unlawfull, which are thinges directly contrary to the symptomes of Melancholie, whereof I spake, and further experience daylie proves how loath they are to confesse without torture, which witnesseth their guiltines, where by the contrary, the Melancholicques never spares to bewray themselves, by their continuall discourses, feeding therby their humor in that which they thinke no crime. As to your third reason, it scarselie merites an answere. For if the devill their master were not bridled, as the scriptures teacheth us, suppose there were no men nor women to be his instrumentes, he could finde waies inough without anie helpe of others to wrack al mankinde: whereunto he employes his whole study, and goeth about like a roaring Lyon (as Peter saith)[2] to that effect, but the limites of his power were set down before the foundations of the world were laid, which he hath not power in the least jote to transgresse. But beside all this, there is over greate a certainty to prove that they are, by the daily experience of the harmes that they do, both to men, and whatsoever thing men possesses, whome God will permit them to be the instrumentes, so to trouble or visite, as in my discourse of that arte, yee shall heare clearelie proved.

2. 1. Pet. 5.

CHAP. II.

ARGUMENT.

The Etymologie and signification of that word of Sorcerie. The first entresse and prentishippe of them that gives themselves to that craft.

Philomathes. Come on then I pray you, and returne where ye left.

Epi. This word of Sorcerie is a Latine worde, which is taken from casting of the lot, & therefore he that useth it, is called Sortiarius à sorte. As to the word of Witchcraft, it is nothing but a proper name given in our language. The cause wherefore they were called sortiarij, proceeded of their practicques seeming to come of lot or chance: Such as the turning of the riddle: the knowing of the forme of prayers, or such like tokens: If a person diseased woulde live or dye. And in generall, that name was given them for using of such charmes, and freites, as that Crafte teacheth them. Manie poynts of their craft and practicques are common]betuixt the Magicians and them: for they serue both one Master, althought in diverse fashions. And as I deuided the Necromancers, into two sorts, learned and unlearned; so must I denie them in other two, riche and of better accompt, poore and of basser degree. These two degrees now of persones, that practises this craft, answers to the passions in them, which (I told you before) the Devil used as meanes to intyse them to his service, for such of them as are in great miserie and povertie, he allures to follow him, by promising unto them greate riches, and worldlie commoditie. Such as though riche, yet burnes in a desperat desire of revenge, hee allures them by promises, to get their turne satisfied to their hartes contentment. It is to be noted nowe, that that olde and craftie enemie of ours, assailes none, though touched with any of these two extremities, except he first finde an entresse reddy for him, either by the great ignorance of the person he deales with, ioyned with an evill life, or else by their carelesnes and contempt of God: And finding them in an utter despair, for one of these two former causes that I have spoken of; he prepares the way by feeding them craftely in their humour, and filling them further and further with despaire, while he finde the time proper to discover himself unto them. At which time, either upon their walking solitarie in the fieldes, or else lying pansing in their bed; but alwaies without the company of any other, he either by a voyce, or in likenesse of a man inquires of them, what troubles them: and promiseth them, a suddaine and certaine waie of remedie, upon condition on the other parte, that they follow his advise; and do such thinges as he wil require of them: Their mindes being prepared before hand, as I have alreadie spoken, they easelie agreed unto that demande of his: And syne settes an other tryist, where they may meete againe. At which time, before he proceede any further with them, he first perswades them to addict themselves to his service: which being easely obteined, he then discovers what he is unto them: makes them to renunce their God and Baptisme directlie, and gives them his marke upon some secreit place of their bodie, which remaines soare unhealed, while his next meeting with them, and thereafter ever insensible, how soever it be nipped or pricked by any, as is dailie proved, to give them a proofe thereby, that as in that doing, hee could hurte and heale them; so all their ill and well doing thereafter, must depende upon him. And besides that, the intollerable dolour that they feele in that place, where he hath marked them, serues to waken them, and not to let them rest, while their next meeting againe: fearing least otherwaies they might either forget him, being as new Prentises, and not well inough founded yet, in that fiendlie follie: or else remembring of that horrible promise they made him, at their last meeting, they might skunner at the same, and preasse to call it back. At their thirde meeting, he makes a shew to be carefull to performe his promises, either by teaching them waies howe to get themselves revenged, if they be of that sort: Or els by teaching them lessons, how by moste vilde and unlawfull meanes, they may obtaine gaine, and worldlie commoditie, if they be of the other sorte.

CHAP. III.

ARGUMENT.

The Witches actiones divided in two partes. The actiones proper to their owne persones. Their actiones toward others. The forme of their conventiones, and adoring of their Master.

Philomathes. Ye have said now inough of their initiating in that ordour. It restes then that ye discourse upon their practises, fra they be passed Prentises: for I would faine heare what is possible to them to performe in verie deede. Although they serue a common Master with the Necromancers, (as I have before saide) yet serue they him in an other forme. For as the meanes are diverse, which allures them to these unlawfull artes of seruing of the Devill; so by diverse waies use they their practises, answering to these meanes, which first the Devill, used as instrumentes in them; though al tending to one end: To wit, the enlargeing of Sathans tyrannie, and crossing of the propagation of the Kingdome of Christ, so farre as lyeth in the possibilitie, either of the one or other sorte, or of the Devill their Master. For where the Magicians, as allured by curiositie, in the most parte of their practises, seekes principallie the satisfying of the same, and to winne to themselves a popular honoure and estimation: These Witches on the other parte, being intised ether for the desire of revenge, or of worldly riches, their whole practises are either to hurte men and their gudes, or what they possesse, for satisfying of their cruell mindes in the former, or else by the wracke in whatsoever sorte, of anie whome God will permitte them to have power off, to satisfie their greedie desire in the last poynt.

Epi. In two partes their actiones may be divided; the actiones of their owne persones, and the actiones proceeding from them towardes anie other. And this division being wel understood, will easilie resolve you, what is possible to them to doe. For although all that they confesse is no lie upon their parte, yet doubtlesly in my opinion, a part of it is not indeede, according as they take it to be: And in this I meane by the actiones of their owne persones. For as I said before, speaking of Magic that the Devill illudes the senses of these schollers of his, in manie thinges, so saye I the like of these Witches.

Phi. Then I pray you, first to speake of that part of their owne persons, and syne ye may come next to their actiones towardes others.

Epi. To the effect that they may performe such services of their false Master, as he employes them in, the devill as Gods Ape, counterfeites in his seruantes this service & forme of adoration, that God prescribed and made his seruantes to practise. For as the seruants of GOD, publicklie uses to conveene for seruing of him, so makes he them in great numbers to conveene (though publickly they dare not) for his service. As none conveenes to the adoration and worshipping of God, except they be marked with his scale, the Sacrament of Baptisme: So none serues Sathan, and conveenes to the adoring of him, that are not marked with that marke, wherof I alredy spake. As the Minister sent by God, teacheth plainely at the time of their publick conventions, how to serue him in spirit & truth: so that uncleane spirite, in his owne person teacheth his Disciples, at the time of their conveening, how to worke all kinde of mischiefe: And craues compt of all their horrible and detestable proceedinges passed, for aduancement of his service. Yea, that he may the more vivelie counterfeit and scorne God, he oft times makes his slaves to conveene in these verrie places, which are destinat and ordeined for the conveening of the servantes of God (I meane by Churches). But this farre, which I have yet said, I not onelie take it to be true in their opiniones, but even so to be indeede. For the forme that he used in counterfeiting God amongst the Gentiles, makes me so to thinke: As God spake by his Oracles, spake he not so by his? As GOD had aswell bloudie Sacrifices, as others without bloud, had not he the like? As God had Churches sanctified to his service, with Altars, Priests, Sacrifices, Ceremonies and Prayers; had he not the like polluted to his service? As God gave responses by Vrim and Thummim, gave he not his responses by the intralls of beastes, by the singing of Fowles, and by their actiones in the aire? As God by visiones, dreames, and extases reveiled what was to come, and what was his will unto his seruantes; used he not the like meanes to forwarne his slaves of things to come? Yea, even as God loued cleannes, hated vice, and impuritie, & appoynted punishmentes therefore: used he not the like (though falselie I grant, and but in eschewing the lesse inconvenient, to draw them upon a greater) yet dissimuled he not I say, so farre as to appoynt his Priestes to keepe their bodies cleane and undefiled, before their asking responses of him? And feyned he not God to be a protectour of everie vertue, and a iust revenger of the contrarie? This reason then moues me, that as he is that same Devill; and as craftie nowe as he was then; so wil hee not spare a pertelie in these actiones that I have spoken of, concerning the witches persones: But further, Witches oft times confesses not only his conveening in the Church with them, but his occupying of the Pulpit: Yea, their forme of adoration, to be the kissing of his hinder partes. Which though it seeme ridiculous, yet may it likewise be true, seeing we reade that in Calicute, he appearing in forme of a Goate-bucke, hath publicklie that un-honest homage done unto him, by everie one of the people: So ambitious is he, and greedie of honour (which procured his fall) that he will even imitate God in that parte, where it is said, that Moyses could see but the hinder partes of God, for the brightnesse of his glorie:[1] And yet that speache is spoken but anthropopathic.

1. Exo. 33.

CHAP. IV.

ARGUMENT.

What are the waies possible, wherby the witches may transport themselves to places far distant, And what ar impossible & mere illusiones of Sathan. And the reasons therof.

Philomathes. But by what way say they or think ye it possible that they can com to these unlawful cōuentiōs?

Epi. There is the thing which I esteeme their senses to be deluded in, and though they lye not in confessing of it, because they thinke it to be true, yet not to be so in substance or effect: for they saie, that by diverse meanes they may conveene, either to the adoring of their Master, or to the putting in practise any service of his, committed unto their charge: one way is natural, which is natural riding, going or sayling, at what houre their Master comes and aduertises them. And this way may be easelie beleved: an other way is some-what more strange: and yet is it possible to be true: which is by being carryed by the force of the Spirite which is their conducter, either aboue the earth or aboue the Sea swiftlie, to the place where they are to meet: which I am perswaded to be likewaies possible, in respect that as Habakkuk was carryed by the Angell in that forme, to the denne where Daniell laie;[1] so thinke I, the Devill will be reddie to imitate God, as well in that as in other thinges: which is much more possible to him to doe, being a Spirite, then to a mighty winde, being but a naturall meteore, to transporte from one place to an other a solide bodie, as is commonlie and dailie seene in practise: But in this violent forme they cannot be carryed, but a shorte boundes, agreeing with the space that they may reteine their breath: for if it were longer, their breath could not remaine unextinguished, their bodie being carryed in such a violent & forceable maner, as be example: If one fall off an small height, his life is but in perrell, according to the harde or soft lighting: But if one fall from an high and stay rocke, his breath wilbe forceablie banished from the bodie, before he can win to the earth, as is oft seen by experience. And in this transporting they say themselves, that they are inuisible to anie other, except amongst themselves; which may also be possible in my opinion. For if the devil may forme what kinde of impressiones he pleases in the aire, as I have said before, speaking of Magie, why may he not far easilier thicken & obscure so the air, that is next about them by contracting it strait together, that the beames of any other mans eyes, cannot pearce thorow the same, to see them? But the third way of their comming to their conventions, is, that where in I think them deluded: for some of them sayeth, that being transformed in the likenesse of a little beast or foule, they will come and pearce through whatsoever house or Church, though all ordinarie passages be closed, by whatsoever open, the aire may enter in at. And some sayeth, that their bodies lying stil as in an extasy, their spirits wil be rauished out of their bodies, & caried to such places. And for verefying therof, wil give euident tokens, aswel by witnesses that have seene their body lying senseles in the

1. Apocrypha of Bell and the Dragon.

meane time, as by naming persones, whom-with they mette, and giuing tokens what purpose was amongst them, whome otherwaies they could not have knowen: for this forme of journeing, they affirme to use most, when they are transported from one Countrie to another.

Phi. Surelie I long to heare your owne opinion of this: For they are like old wives trattles about the fire. The reasons that moues me to thinke that these are meere illusiones, ar these. First for them that are transformed in likenes of beastes or foules, can enter through so narrow passages, although I may easelie beleeve that the Devill coulde by his woorkemanshippe upon the aire, make them appeare to be in such formes, either to themselves or to others: Yet how he can contract a solide bodie within so little roome, I thinke it is directlie contrarie to it selfe, for to be made so little, and yet not diminished: To be so straitlie drawen together, and yet feele no paine; I thinke it is so contrarie to the qualitie of a naturall bodie, and so like to the little transubstantiat god in the Papistes Masse, that I can never beleeve it. So to have a quantitie, is so proper to a solide bodie, that as all Philosophers conclude, it cannot be any more without one, then a spirite can have one. For when Peter came out of the prison,[2] and the doores all locked: It was not by any contracting of his bodie in so little roome: but by the giuing place of the dore, though un-espyed by the Gaylors. And yet is there no comparison, when this is done, betuixt the power of God, and of the Devill. As to their forme of extasie and spirituall transporting, it is certaine the soules going out of the bodie, is the onely difinition of naturall death: and who are once dead, God forbid wee should thinke that it should lie in the power of all the Devils in Hell, to restore them to their life againe: Although he can put his owne spirite in a dead

2. Act. 12.

bodie, which the Necromancers commonlie practise, as yee have harde. For that is the office properly belonging to God; and besides that, the soule once parting from the bodie, cannot wander anie longer in the worlde, but to the owne resting place must it goe immediatlie, abiding the conjunction of the bodie againe, at the latter daie. And what Christ or the Prophets did miraculouslie in this case, it cannot in no Christian mans opinion be maid common with the Devill. As for anie tokens that they give for proouing of this, it is verie possible to the Devils craft, to perswade them to these meanes. For he being a spirite, may hee not so rauishe their thoughtes, and dull their sences, that their bodie lying as dead, hee may object to their spirites as it were in a dreame, & (as the Poets write of Morpheus) represente such formes of persones, of places, and other circumstances, as he pleases to illude them with? Yea, that he maie deceive them with the greater efficacie, may hee not at that same instant, by fellow angelles of his, illude such other persones so in that same fashion, whome with he makes them to beleeve that they mette; that all their reportes and tokens, though severallie examined, may everie one agree with an other. And that whatsoever actiones, either in hurting men or beasts: or whatsoever other thing that they falselie imagine, at that time to have done, may by himselfe or his marrowes, at that same time be done indeede; so as if they would give for a token of their being rauished at the death of such a person within so shorte space thereafter, whom they beleeve to have poysoned, or witched at that instante, might hee not at that same houre, have smitten that same person by the permission of GOD, to the farther deceiving of them, and to mooue others to beleeve them? And this is surelie the likeliest way, and most according to reason, which my judgement can finde out in this, and whatsoever other unnaturall poyntes of their confession. And by these meanes shall we saill surelie, betuixt Charybdis and Scylla, in eschewing the not beleeuing of them altogether on the one part, least that drawe us to the errour that there is no Witches: and on the other parte in beleeuing of it, make us to eschew the falling into innumerable absurdities, both monstruouslie against all Theologie divine, and Philosophie humaine.

CHAP. V.

ARGUMENT.

Witches actiones towardes others. Why there are more women of that craft nor men? What thinges are possible to them to effectuate by the power of their master. The reasons thereof. What is the surest remedie of the harmes done by them.

Philomathes. Forsooth your opinion in this, seemes to carrie most reason with it, and sence yee have ended, then the actions belonging properly to their owne persones: say forwarde now to their actiones used towardes others.

Epi. In their actiones used towardes others, three thinges ought to be considered: First the maner of their consulting thereupon: Next their part as instrumentes: And last their masters parte, who puts the same in execution. As to their consultationes thereupon, they use them oftest in the Churches, where they conveene for adoring: at what time their master enquiring at them what they would be at: everie one of them propones unto him, what wicked turne they would have done, either for obteining of riches, or for revenging them upon anie whome they have malice at: who granting their demande, as no doubt willinglie he wil, since it is to doe evill, he teacheth them the means, wherby they may do the same. As for little trifling turnes that women have ado with, he causeth them to ioynt dead corpses, & to make powders thereof, mixing such other thinges there amongst, as he gives unto them.

Phi. But before yee goe further, permit mee I pray you to interrupt you one worde, which yee have put mee in memorie of, by speaking of Women. What can be the cause that there are twentie women given to that craft, where ther is one man?

Epi. The reason is easie, for as that sexe is frailer then man is, so is it easier to be intrapped in these grosse snares of the Devill, as was over well proved to be true, by the Serpents deceiving of Eua at the beginning, which makes him the homelier with that sexe sensine.

Phi. Returne now where ye left.

Epi. To some others at these times hee teacheth how to make Pictures of waxe or clay: That by the rosting thereof, the persones that they beare the name of, may be continuallie melted or dryed awaie by continuall sicknesse. To some hee gives such stones or poulders, as will helpe to cure or cast on diseases: And to some he teacheth kindes of uncouthe poysons, which Mediciners understandes not (for he is farre cunningner then man in the knowledge of all the occult proprieties of nature) not that anie of these meanes which hee teacheth them (except the poysons which are composed of thinges naturall) can of them selveshelpe any thing to these turnes, that they are employed in, but onelie being Gods Ape, as well in that, as in all other thinges. Even as God by his Sacramentes which are earthlie of themselves workes a heavenlie effect, though no waies by any cooperation in them: And as Christ by clay & spettle wrought together, opened the eies of the blynd man,[1] suppose there was no vertue in that which he outwardlie applyed, so the Devill will have his out-warde meanes to be shewes as it were of his doing, which hath no part of cooperation in his turnes with him, how farre that ever the ignorantes be abused in the contrarie. And as to the effectes of these two former partes, to wit, the consultationes and the outward meanes, they are so wounderfull as I dare not allege anie of them, without ioyning a sufficient reason of the possibilitie thereof. For leauing all the small trifles among wives, and to speake of the principall poyntes of their craft. For the common trifles thereof, they can do without converting well inough by themselves: These principall poyntes I say are these: They can make men or women to loue or hate other, which may be verie possible to the Devil to effectual, seing he being a subtile spirite, knowes well inough how to perswade the corrupted affection of them whom God will permit him so to deale with: They can lay the siknesse of one upon an other, which likewise is verie possible unto him: For since by Gods permission, he layed siknesse upon Iob, why may he not farre easilier lay it upon any other: For as an old practisian, he knowes well inough what humor domines most in anie of us, and as a spirite hee can subtillie walken up the same, making it peccant, or to abounde, as he thinkes meete for troubling of us, when God will so permit him. And for the taking off of it, no doubt he will be glad to relive such of present paine, as he may thinke by these meanes to perswade to bee catched in his everlasting snares and fetters. They can be-witch and take the life of men or women, by rosting of the Pictures, as I spake of before, which likewise is verie possible to their Master to performe, for although, (as I saide before) that instrumente of waxe have no vertue in that turne doing,

1. John. 9.

yet may hee not verie well even by that same measure that his conjured slaves meltes that waxe at the fire, may he not I say at these same times, subtilie as a spirite so weaken and scatter the spirites of life of the patient, as may make him on th'one part, for faintnesse to sweate out the humour of his bodie: And on the other parte, for the not concurrence of these spirites, which causes his digestion, so debilitat his stomak, that his humour radicall continually, sweating out on the one parte, and no new good suck being put in the place thereof, for lack of digestion on the other, hee at last shall vanish awaie, even as his picture will doe at the fire. And that knauish and cunning woorkeman, by troubling him onely at some times, makes a proportion so neare betuixt the woorking of the one and the other, that both shall ende as it were at one time. They can rayse stormes and tempestes in the aire, either upon Sea or land, though not universally, but in such a particular place and prescribed boundes, as God will permitte them so to trouble: Which likewise is verie easie to be discerned from anie other naturall tempestes that are meteores, in respect of the suddaine and violent raising thereof, together with the short induring of the same. And this is likewise verie possible to their master to do, he having such affinitie with the aire as being a spirite, and having such power of the forming and moouing thereof, as ye have heard me alreadie declare: For in the Scripture, that stile of the Prince of the aire is given unto him.[2] They can make folkes to becom phrenticque or Maniacque, which likewise is very possible to their master to do, sence they are but naturall sicknesses: and so he may lay on these kindes, aswell as anie others. They can make spirites either to follow and trouble persones, or haunt certaine houses, and affraie oftentimes the inhabitantes: as hath bene knowen to be done by our Witches at this time. And likewise they can make some to be possessed

2. Ephes. 2.

with spirites, & so to becom verie Dæmoniacques: and this last sorte is verie possible likewise to the Devill their Master to do, since he may easilie send his owne angells to trouble in what forme he pleases, any whom God wil permit him so to use.

Phi. But will God permit these wicked instrumentes by the power of the Devill their master, to trouble by anie of these meanes, anie that beleeves in him?

Epi. No doubt, for there are three kinde of folkes whom God will permit so to be tempted or troubled; the wicked for their horrible sinnes, to punish them in the like measure; The godlie that are sleeping in anie great sinnes or infirmities and weakenesse in faith, to waken them up the faster by such an uncouth forme: and even some of the best, that their patience may bee tryed before the world, as Jobs was. For why may not God use anie kinde of extraordinarie punishment, when it pleases him; as well as the ordinarie roddes of sicknesse or other adversities.

Phi. Who then may be free from these Devilish practises?

Epi. No man ought to presume so far as to promise anie impunitie to himselfe: for God hath before all beginninges preordinated aswell the particular sortes of Plagues as of benefites for everie man, which in the owne time he ordaines them to be visited with, & yet ought we not to be the more affrayde for that, of any thing that the Devill and his wicked instrumentes can do against us: For we dailie fight against the Devill in a hundreth other waies: And therefore as a valiant Captaine, affraies no more being at the combat, nor stayes from his purpose for the rummishing shot of a Cannon, nor the small clack of a Pistolet: suppose he be not certaine what may light upon him; Even so ought we boldlie to goe forwarde in fighting against the Devill without anie greater terrour, for these his rarest weapons, nor for the ordinarie whereof wee have daily the proofe.

Phi. Is it not lawfull then by the helpe of some other Witche to cure the disease that is casten on by that craft?

Epi. No waies lawfull: For I gave you the reason thereof in that axiome of Theologie, which was the last wordes I spake of Magie.

Phi. How then may these diseases be lawfullie cured?

Epi. Onelie by earnest prayer to GOD, by amendement of their lives, and by sharp persewing everie one, according to his calling of these instrumentes of Sathan, whose punishment to the death will be a salutarie sacrifice for the patient. And this is not onely the lawfull way, but likewise the most sure: For by the Devils meanes, can never the Devill be casten out, as Christ sayeth.[3] And when such a cure is used, it may wel serue for a shorte time, but at the last, it will doubtleslie tend to the utter perdition of the patient, both in bodie and soule.

3. Mark. 3.

CHAP. VI.

ARGUMENT.

What sorte of folkes are least or most subiect to receive harme by Witchcraft. What power they have to harme the Magistrate, and upon what respectes they have any power in prison: And to what end may or will the Devill appeare to them therein. Upon what respectes the Devill appeires in sundry shapes to s undry of them at any time.

Philomathes. But who dare take upon him to punish them, if no man can be sure to be free from their unnaturall inuasiones?

Epi. We ought not the more of that restraine from vertue, that the way wherby we climbe thereunto be straight and perrilous. But besides that, as there is no kinde of persones so subject to receive harme of them, as these that are of infirme and weake faith (which is the best buckler against such inuasiones:) so have they so smal power over none, as over such as zealouslie and earnestlie persewes them, without sparing for anie worldlie respect.

Phi. Then they are like the Pest, which smites these sickarest,

that flies it farthest, and apprehends deepliest the perrell thereof.
Epi. It is even so with them: For neither is it able to them to use anie false cure upon a patient, except the patient first beleeve in their power, and so hazard the tinsell of his owne soule, nor yet can they have lesse power to hurte anie, nor such as contemnes most their doinges, so being it comes of faith, and not of anie vaine arrogancie in themselves.

Phi. But what is their power against the Magistrate?

Epi. Lesse or greater, according as he deales with them. For if he be slouthfull towardes them, God is verie able to make them instrumentes to waken & punish his slouth. But if he be the contrarie, he according to the iust law of God, and allowable law of all Nationes, will be diligent in examining and punishing of them: GOD will not permit their master to trouble or hinder so good a woorke.

Phi. But fra they be once in handes and firmance, have they anie further power in their craft?

Epi. That is according to the forme of their detention. If they be but apprehended and deteined by anie private person, upon other private respectes, their power no doubt either in escaping, or in doing hurte, is no lesse nor ever it was before. But if on the other parte, their apprehending and detention be by the lawfull Magistrate, upon the iust respectes of their guiltinesse in that craft, their power is then no greater then before that ever they medled with their master. For where God beginnes iustlie to strike by his lawfull Lieutennentes, it is not in the Devilles power to defraude or bereaue him of the office, or effect of his powerfull and revenging Scepter.

Phi. But will never their master come to visite them, fra they be once apprehended and put in firmance?

Epi. That is according to the estaite that these miserable wretches are in: For if they be obstinate in still denying, he will not spare, when he findes time to speake with them, either if he finde them in anie comfort, to fill them more and more with the vaine hope of some maner of reliefe: or else if hee finde them in a deepe dispaire, by all meanes to augment the same, and to perswade them by some extraordinarie meanes to put themselves downe, which verie commonlie they doe. But if they be penitent and confesse, God will not permit him to trouble them anie more with his presence and allurementes.

Phi. It is not good using his counsell I see then. But I woulde earnestlie know when he appeares to them in Prison, what formes uses he then to take?

Epi. Divers formes, even as he uses to do at other times unto them. For as I told you, speking of Magie, he appeares to that kinde of craftes-men ordinarily in an forme, according as they agree upon it amongst themselves: Or if they be but prentises, according to the qualitie of their circles or conjurationes: Yet to these capped creatures, he appeares as he pleases, and as he findes meetest for their humors. For even at their publick conventiones, he appeares to divers of them in divers formes, as we have found by the difference of their confessiones in that point: For he deluding them with vaine impressiones in the aire, makes himselfe to seeme more terrible to the grosser sorte, that they maie thereby be moued to feare and reverence him the more: And les monstrous and uncouthlike againe to the craftier sorte, least otherwaies they might sturre and skunner at his uglinesse.

Phi. How can he then be felt, as they confesse they have done him, if his bodie be but of aire?

Epi. I heare little of that amongst their confessiones, yet may he make himselfe palpable, either by assuming any dead bodie, and using the ministrie thereof, or else by deluding as wel their sence of feeling as seeing; which is not impossible to him to doe, since all our senses, as we are so weake, and even by ordinarie sicknesses will be often times deluded.

Phi. But I would speere one worde further yet, concerning his appearing to them in prison, which is this. May any other that chances to be present at that time in the prison, see him as well as they.

Epi. Some-times they will, and some-times not, as it pleases God.

CHAP. VII.

ARGUMENT.

Two formes of the devils visible conversing in the earth, with the reasones wherefore the one of them was communest in the time of Papistrie: And the other sensine. Those that denies the power of the Devill, denies the power of God, and are guiltie of the errour of the Sadduces.

Philomathes. Hath the Devill then power to appeare to any other, except to such as are his sworne disciples: especially since al Oracles, & such like kinds of illusiones were taken awaie and abolished by the cumming of Christ?

Epi. Although it be true indeede, that the brightnesse of the Gospell at his cumming, scaled the cloudes of all these grosse errors in the Gentilisme: yet that these abusing spirites, ceases not sensine at sometimes to appeare, dailie experience teaches us. Indeede this difference is to be marked betwixt the formes of Sathans conversing visiblie in the world. For of two different formes thereof, the one of them by the spreading of the Euangell, and conquest of the white horse, in the sixt Chapter of the Revelation, is much hindred and become rarer there through. This his appearing to any Christians, troubling of them outwardly, or possessing of them constraynedly. The other of them is become communer and more used sensine, I meane by their unlawfull artes, whereupon our whole purpose hath bene. This we finde by experience in this Ile to be true. For as we know, moe Ghostes and spirites were seene, nor tongue can tell, in the time of blinde Papistrie in these Countries, where now by the contrarie, a man shall scarcely all his time here once of such things. And yet were these unlawfull artes farre rarer at that time: and never were so much harde of, nor so rife as they are now.

Phi. What should be the cause of that?

Epi. The diverse nature of our sinnes procures at the Iustice of God, diverse sortes of punishments answering thereunto. And therefore as in the time of Papistrie, our fathers erring grosselie, & through ignorance, that mist of errours overshaddowed the Devill to walke the more familiarlie amongst them: And as it were by barnelie and affraying terroures, to mocke and accuse their barnelie erroures. By the contrarie, we now being sounde of Religion, and in our life rebelling to our profession, God iustlie by that sinne of rebellion, as Samuel calleth it, accuseth our life so wilfullie fighting against our profession.

Phi. Since yee are entred now to speake of the appearing of spirites: I would be glad to heare your opinion in that matter. For manie denies that anie such spirites can appeare in these daies as I have said.

Epi. Doubtleslie who denyeth the power of the Devill, woulde likewise denie the power of God, if they could for shame. For since the Devill is the verie contrarie opposite to God, there can be no better way to know God, then by the contrarie; as by the ones power (though a creature) to admire the power of the great Creator: by the falshood of the one to considder the trueth of the other, by the injustice of the one, to considder the Iustice of the other: And by the cruelty of the one, to considder the mercifulnesse of the other: And so foorth in all the rest of the essence of God, and qualities of the Devill. But I feare indeede, there be over many Sadduces in this worlde, that denies all kindes of spirites: For convicting of whose errour, there is cause inough if there were no more, that God should permit at sometimes spirits visiblie to kyith.

THIRDE BOOKE.

ARGUMENT.

THE DESCRIPTION OF ALL THESE KINDES OF SPIRITES THAT TROUBLES MEN OR WOMEN. THE CONCLUSION OF THE WHOLE DIALOGUE.

CHAP. I.

ARGUMENT.

The division of spirites in foure principall kindes. The description of the first kinde of them, called Spectra & vmbræ mortuorum. What is the best way to be free of their trouble.

Philomathes. I pray you now then go forward in telling what ye thinke fabulous, or may be trowed in that case.

Epi. That kinde of the Devils conversing in the earth, may be divided in foure different kindes, whereby he affrayeth and troubleth the bodies of men: For of the abusing of the soule, I have spoken alreadie. The first is, where spirites troubles some houses or solitarie places: The second, where spirites followes upon certaine persones, and at divers houres troubles them: The thirde, when they enter within them and possesse them: The fourth is these kinde of spirites that are called vulgarlie the Fayrie. Of the three former kindes, ye harde alreadie, how they may artificiallie be made by Witch-craft to trouble folke: Now it restes to speake of their naturall comming as it were, and not raysed by Witch-craft. But generally I must for-warne you of one thing before I enter in this purpose: that is, that although in my discourseing of them, I deuyde them in divers kindes, yee must notwithstanding there of note my Phrase of speaking in that: For doubtleslie they are in effect, but all one kinde of spirites, who for abusing the more of mankinde, takes on these sundrie shapes, and uses diverse formes of out-ward actiones, as if some were of nature better then other. Nowe I returne to my purpose: As to the first kinde of these spirites, that were called by the auncients by divers names, according as their actions were. For if they were spirites that haunted some houses, by appearing in divers and horrible formes, and making greate dinne: they were called Lemures or Spectra. If they appeared in likenesse of anie defunct to some friends of his, they wer called vmbræ mortuorum: And so innumerable stiles they got, according to their actiones, as I have said alreadie. As we see by experience, how manie stiles they have given them in our language in the like maner: Of the appearing of these spirites, wee are certified by the Scriptures,[1] where the Prophet Esay 13. and 34. cap. threatning the destruction of Babell and Edom: declares, that it shal not onlie be wracked, but shall become so greate a solitude, as it shall be the habitackle of Howlettes, and of Ziim and Iim, which are the proper Hebrewe names for these Spirites. The cause whie they haunte solitarie places, it is by reason, that they may affraie and brangle the more the faith of suche as them alone hauntes such places. For our nature is such, as in companies wee are not so soone mooued to anie such kinde of feare, as being solitare, which the Devill knowing well inough, hee will not therefore assaile us but when we are weake: And besides that, GOD will not permit him so to dishonour the societies and companies of Christians, as in publicke times and places to walke visiblie amongst them. On the other parte, when he troubles certaine houses that are dwelt in, it is a sure token either of grosse ignorance, or of some grosse

1.Esay. 13. Jere. 50.

and slanderous sinnes amongst the inhabitantes thereof: which God by that extraordinarie rod punishes.

Phi. But by what way or passage can these Spirites enter in these houses, seeing they alledge that they will enter, Doore and Window being steiked?

Epi. They will choose the passage for their entresse, according to the forme that they are in at that time. For if they have assumed a deade bodie, whereinto they lodge themselves, they can easely inough open without dinne anie Doore or Window, and enter in thereat. And if they enter as a spirite onelie, anie place where the aire may come in at, is large inough an entrie for them: For as I said before, a spirite can occupie no quantitie.

Phi. And will God then permit these wicked spirites to trouble the reste of a dead bodie, before the resurrection thereof? Or if he will so, I thinke it should be of the reprobate onely.

Epi. What more is the reste troubled of a dead bodie, when the Devill carryes it out of the Graue to serue his turne for a space, nor when the Witches takes it up and joyntes it, or when as Swine wortes uppe the graues? The rest of them that the Scripture speakes of, is not meaned by a locall remaining continuallie in one place, but by their resting from their trauelles and miseries of this worlde, while their latter conjunction againe with the soule at that time to receaue full glorie in both. And that the Devill may use aswell the ministrie of the bodies of the faithfull in these cases, as of the un-faithfull, there is no inconvenient; for his haunting with their bodies after they are deade, can no-waies defyle them: In respect of the soules absence. And for anie dishonour it can be unto them, by what reason can it be greater, then the hanging, heading, or many such shameful deaths, that good men will suffer? for there is nothing in the bodies of the faithfull, more worthie of honour, or freer from corruption by nature, nor in these of the unfaithful, while time they be purged and glorified in the latter daie, as is dailie seene by the vilde diseases and corruptions, that the bodies of the faythfull are subject unto, as yee will see clearelie proved, when I speake of the possessed and Dæmoniacques.

Phi. Yet there are sundrie that affirmes to have haunted such places, where these spirites are alleaged to be: And coulde never heare nor see anie thing.

Epi. I thinke well: For that is onelie reserued to the secreete knowledge of God, whom he wil permit to see such thinges, and whome not.

Phi. But where these spirites hauntes and troubles anie houses, what is the best waie to banishe them?

Epi. By two meanes may onelie the remeid of such things be procured: The one is ardent prayer to God, both of these persones that are troubled with them, and of that Church whereof they are. The other is the purging of themselves by amendement of life from such sinnes, as have procured that extraordinarie plague.

Phi. And what meanes then these kindes of spirites, when they appeare in the shaddow of a person newlie dead, or to die, to his friendes?

Epi. When they appeare upon that occasion, they are called Wraithes in our language. Amongst the Gentiles the Devill used that much, to make them beleeve that it was some good spirite that appeared to them then, ether to forewarne them of the death of their friend; or else to discover unto them, the will of the defunct, or what was the way of his slauchter, as is written in the booke of the histories Prodigious. And this way hee easelie deceived the Gentiles, because they knew not God: And to that same effect is it, that he now appeares in that maner to some ignorant Christians. For he dare not so illude anie that knoweth that, neither can the spirite of the defunct returne to his friend, or yet an Angell use such formes.

Phi. And are not our war-woolfes one sorte of these spirits also, that hauntes and troubles some houses or dwelling places?

Epi. There hath indeede bene an old opinion of such like thinges; For by the Greekes they were called werewolf which signifieth men-woolfes. But to tell you simplie my opinion in this, if anie such thing hath bene, I take it to have proceeded but of a naturall super-abundance of Melancholie, which as wee reade, that it hath made some thinke themselves Pitchers, and some horses, and some one kinde of beast or other: So suppose I that it hath so viciat the imagination and memorie of some, as per lucida interualla, it hath so highlie occupyed them, that they have thought themselves verrie Woolfes indeede at these times: and so have counterfeited their actiones in goeing on their handes and feete, preassing to deuoure women and barnes, fighting and snatching with all the towne dogges, and in using such like other bruitish actiones, and so to become beastes by a strong apprehension, as Nebucad-netzar was seven yeares:[2] but as to their having and hyding of their hard & schellie sloughes, I take that to be but eiked, by uncertaine report, the author of all lyes.

2. Dan. 4.

CHAP. II.

ARGUMENT.

The description of the next two kindes of Spirites, whereof the one followes outwardlie, the other possesses inwardlie the persones that they trouble. That since all Prophecies and visiones are nowe ceased, all spirites that appeares in these formes are evill.

Philomathes. Come forward now to the reste of these kindes of spirites.

Epi. As to the next two kindes, that is, either these that outwardlie troubles and followes some persones, or else inwardlie possesses them: I will conjoyne them in one, because aswel the causes ar alike in the persons that they are permitted to trouble: as also the waies whereby they may be remedied and cured.

Phi. What kinde of persones are they that uses to be so troubled?

Epi. Two kindes in speciall: Either such as being guiltie of greeuous offences, God punishes by that horrible kinde of scourdge, or else being persones of the beste nature peraduenture, that yee shall finde in all the Countrie about them, GOD permittes them to be troubled in that sort, for the tryall of their patience, and wakening up of their zeale, for admonishing of the beholders, not to truste over much in themselves, since they are made of no better stuffe, and peraduenture blotted with no smaller sinnes (as Christ saide, speaking of them uppon whome the Towre in Siloam fell)[1] And for giuing likewise to the spectators, matter to prayse GOD, that they meriting no better, are yet spared from being corrected in that fearefull forme.

Phi. These are good reasones for the parte of GOD, which apparantlie mooues him so to permit the Devill to trouble such persones. But since the Devil hath ever a contrarie respecte in all the actiones that GOD employes him in: which is I pray you the end and mark he shoots at in this turne?

Epi. It is to obtaine one of two thinges thereby, if he may: The one is the tinsell of their life, by inducing them to such perrilous places at such time as he either followes or possesses them, which may procure the same: And such like, so farre as GOD will permit him, by tormenting them to weaken their bodie, and caste them in incurable diseases. The other thinge that hee preases to obteine by troubling of them, is the tinsell of their soule, by intising them to mistruste and blaspheme God: Either for the intollerablenesse of their tormentes, as he assayed to have done with Job;[2] or else for his promising unto them to leave the troubling of them, incase they would so do, as is knowen by experience at this same time by the confession of a young one that was so troubled.

Phi. Since ye have spoken now of both these kindes of spirites

1. Luc. 13.

2. Job. i.

comprehending them in one: I must nowe goe backe againe in speering some questions of everie one of these kindes in speciall. And first for these that followes certaine persones, yee know that there are two sortes of them: One sorte that troubles and tormentes the persones that they haunt with: An other sort that are serviceable unto them in all kinde of their necessaries, and omittes never to forwarne them of anie suddaine perrell that they are to be in. And so in this case, I would understande whither both these sortes be but wicked and damned spirites: Or if the last sorte be rather Angells, (as should appeare by their actiones) sent by God to assist such as he speciallie favoures. For it is written in the Scriptures,[3] that God sendes Legions of Angels to guarde and watch over his elect.

Epi. I know well inough where fra that errour which ye alleage hath proceeded: For it was the ignorant Gentiles that were the fountaine thereof. Who for that they knew not God, they forged in their owne imaginationes, every man to be still accompanied with two spirites, whereof they called the one genius bonus, the other genius malus: the Greekes called them Bliss & Mischief: wherof the former they saide, perswaded him to all the good he did: the other entised him to all the evill. But praised be God we that are christians, & walks not amongst the Cymmerian conjectures of man, knowes well inough, that it is the good spirite of God onely, who is the fountain of all goodnes, that perswads us to the thinking or doing of any good: and that it is our corrupted fleshe and Sathan, that intiseth us to the contrarie. And yet the Devill for confirming in the heades of ignoraunt Christians, that errour first mainteined among the Gentiles, he whiles among the first kinde of spirits that I speak of, appeared in time of Papistrie and blindnesse, and haunted divers houses, without doing any evill, but doing as it were

3. Gen. 32. 1. Kin. 6.Psal. 34.

necessarie turnes up and down the house: and this spirit they called Brownie in our language, who appeared like a rough-man: yea, some were so blinded, as to beleeve that their house was all the sonsier, as they called it, that such spirites resorted there.

Phi. But since the Devils intention in all his actions, is ever to do evill, what evill was there in that forme of doing, since their actions outwardly were good.

Epi. Was it not evill inough to deceive simple ignorantes, in making them to take him for an Angell of light, and so to account of Gods enemie, as of their particular friend: where by the contrarie, all we that are Christians, ought assuredly to know that since the comming of Christ in the flesh, and establishing of his Church by the Apostles, all miracles, visions, prophecies, & appearances of Angels or good spirites are ceased. Which serued onely for the first sowing of faith, & planting of the Church. Where now the Church being established, and the white Horse whereof I spake before, having made his conqueste, the Lawe and Prophets are thought sufficient to serue us, or make us inexcusable, as Christ saith in his parable of Lazarus and the riche man.[4]

4. Luk. 16.

CHAP. III.

ARGUMENT.

The description of a particular sort of that kind of following spirites, called Incubi and Succubi: And what is the reason wherefore these kindes of spirites hauntes most the Northeme and barbarous partes of the world.

Philomathes. The next question that I would speere, is likewise concerning this first of these two kindes of spirites that ye have conjoyned: and it is this; ye knowe how it is commonly written and reported, that amongst the rest of the sortes of spirites that followes certaine persons, there is one more monstrous nor al the rest: in respect as it is alleaged, they converse naturally with them whom they trouble and hauntes with: and therefore I would knowe in two thinges your opinion herein: First if suche a thing can be: and next if it be: whether there be a difference of sexes amongst these spirites or not.

Epi. That abhominable kinde of the Devils abusing of men or women, was called of old, Incubi and Succubi, according to the difference of the sexes that they conversed with. By two meanes this great kinde of abuse might possibly be performed: The one, when the Devill onelie as a spirite, and stealing out the sperme of a dead bodie, abuses them that way, they not graithlie seeing anie shape or feeling anie thing, but that which he so convayes in that part: As we reade of a Monasterie of Nunnes which were burnt for their being that way abused. The other meane is when he borrowes a dead bodie and so visiblie, and as it seemes unto them naturallie as a man converses with them. But it is to be noted, that in whatsoever way he useth it, that sperme seemes intollerably cold to the person abused. For if he steale out the nature of a quick person, it cannot be so quicklie carryed, but it will both tine the strength and heate by the way, which it could never have had for lacke of agitation, which in the time of procreation is the procurer & wakener up of these two natural qualities. And if he occupying the dead bodie as his lodging expell the same out thereof in the dewe time, it must likewise be colde by the participation with the qualities of the dead bodie whereout of it comes. And whereas yee inquire if these spirites be divided in sexes or not, I thinke the rules of Philosophie may easelie resolve a man of the contrarie: For it is a sure principle of that arte, that nothing can be divided in sexes, except such liuing bodies as must have a naturall seede to genere by. But we know spirites hath no seede proper to themselves, nor yet can they gender one with an other.

Phi. How is it then that they say sundrie monsters have bene gotten by that way.

Epi. These tales are nothing but Aniles fabulæ. For that they have no nature of their owne, I have shewed you alreadie. And that the cold nature of a dead bodie, can woorke nothing in generation, it is more nor plaine, as being already dead of it selfe as well as the rest of the bodie is, wanting the naturall heate, and such other naturall operation, as is necessarie for woorking that effect, and incase such a thing were possible (which were all utterly against all the rules of nature) it would breed no monster, but onely such a naturall of-spring, as would have cummed betuixt that man or woman and that other abused person, in-case they both being alive had had a doe with other. For the Devilles parte therein, is but the naked carrying or expelling of that substance: And so it coulde not participate with no qualitie of the same. Indeede, it is possible to the craft of the Devill to make a womans bellie to swel after he hath that way abused her, which he may do, either by steiring up her own humor, or by herbes, as we see beggars daily doe. And when the time of her delivery should come to make her thoil great doloures, like unto that naturall course, and then subtillie to slippe in the Mid-wives handes, stockes, stones, or some monstruous barne brought from some other place, but this is more reported and gessed at by others, nor beleeved by me.

Phi. But what is the cause that this kinde of abuse is thought to be most common in such wild partes of the worlde, as Lap-land, and Fin-land, or in our North Iles of Orknay and Schet-land.

Epi. Because where the Devill findes greatest ignorance and barbaritie, there assayles he grosseliest, as I gave you the reason wherefore there was moe Witches of women kinde nor men.

Phi. Can anie be so unhappie as to give their willing consent to the Devilles vilde abusing them in this forme.

Epi. Yea, some of the Witches have confessed, that he hath perswaded them to give their willing consent thereunto, that he may thereby have them feltred the sikarer in his snares; But as the other compelled sorte is to be pittied and prayed for, so is this most highlie to be punished and detested.

Phi. It is not the thing which we cal the Mare, which takes folkes sleeping in their bedds, a kinde of these spirites, whereof ye are speaking?

Epi. No, that is but a naturall sicknes, which the Mediciners hath given that name of Incubus unto ab incubando, because it being a thicke fleume, falling into our breast upon the harte, while we are sleeping, intercludes so our vitall spirites, and takes all power from us, as maks us think that there were some unnaturall burden or spirite, lying upon us and holding us downe.

CHAP. IV.

ARGUMENT.

The description of the Dæmoniackes & possessed. By what reason the Papistes may have power to cure them.

Philomathes. Wel, I have told you now all my doubts, and ye have satisfied me therein, concerning the first of these two kindes of spirites that ye have conjoyned. Now I am to inquire onely two thinges at you concerning the last kinde, I meane the Dæmoniackes. The first is, whereby shal these possessed folks be discerned fra them that ar trubled with a natural Phrensie or Manie. The next is, how can it be that they can be remedied by the Papistes Church, whome wee counting as Hereticques, it should appeare that one Devil should not cast out an other,[1] for then would his kingdome be divided in it selfe, as Christ said.

Epi. As to your first question; there are divers symptomes, whereby that heauie trouble may be discerned from a naturall sickenesse, and speciallie three, omitting the divers vaine signes that the Papistes attributes unto it: Such as the raging at holie water, their fleeing a back from the Croce, their not abiding

1. Mat. 12. Mark. 3.

the hearing of God named, and innumerable such like vaine thinges that were alike fashious and feckles to recite. But to come to these three symptomes then, whereof I spake, I account the one of them to be the incredible strength of the possessed creature, which will farre exceede the strength of six of the wightest and wodest of any other men that are not so troubled. The next is the boldning up so far of the patients breast and bellie, with such an unnaturall sturring and vehement agitation within them: And such an ironie hardnes of his sinnowes so stiffelie bended out, that it were not possible to prick out as it were the skinne of anie other person so far: so mightely works the Devil in all the members and senses of his body, he being locallie within the same, suppose of his soule and affectiones thereof, hee have no more power then of any other mans. The last is, the speaking of sundrie languages, which the patient is knowen by them that were acquainte with him never to have learned, and that with an uncouth and hollowe voice, and al the time of his speaking, a greater motion being in his breast then in his mouth. But fra this last symptome is excepted such, as are altogether in the time of their possessing bereft of al their senses being possessed with a dumme and blynde spirite, whereof Christ releived one, in the 12. of Mathew. And as to your next demande, it is first to be doubted if the Papistes or anie not professing the the onelie true Religion, can relieve anie of that trouble. And next, in-case they can, upon what respectes it is possible unto them. As to the former upon two reasons, it is grounded: first that it is knowen so manie of them to bee counterfite, which wyle the Clergie inuentes for confirming of their rotten Religion. The next is, that by experience we finde that few, who are possessed indeede, are fullie cured by them: but rather the Devill is content to release the bodelie hurting of them, for a shorte space, thereby to obteine the perpetual hurt of the soules of so many that by these false miracles may be induced or confirmed in the profession of that erroneous Religion: even as I told you before that he doth in the false cures, or casting off of diseases by Witches. As to the other part of the argument in-case they can, which rather (with reverence of the learned thinking otherwaies) I am induced to beleeve, by reason of the faithfull report that men sound of religion, have made according to their sight thereof, I think if so be, I say these may be the respectes, whereupon the Papistes may have that power. Christ gave a commission and power to his Apostles to cast out Devilles, which they according thereunto put in execution: The rules he bad them observe in that action, was fasting and praier: & the action it selfe to be done in his name. This power of theirs proceeded not then of anie vertue in them, but onely in him who directed them. As was clearly proved by Iudas his having as greate power in that commission, as anie of the reste. It is easie then to be understand that the casting out of Devilles, is by the vertue of fasting and prayer, and in-calling of the name of God, suppose manie imperfectiones be in the person that is the instrumente,[2] as Christ him selfe teacheth us of the power that false Prophets sall have to caste out Devils. It is no wounder then, these respects of this action being considered, that it may be possible to the Papistes, though erring in sundrie points of Religion to accomplish this, if they use the right forme prescribed by Christ herein. For what the worse is that action that they erre in other thinges, more then their Baptisme is the worse that they erre in the other Sacrament, and have eiked many vaine freittes to the Baptisme it selfe.

Phi. Surelie it is no little wonder that God should permit the bodies of anie of the faithfull to be so dishonoured, as to be a dwelling place to that uncleane spirite.

2. Mat. 7.

Epi. There is it which I told right now, would proove and strengthen my argument of the devils entring in the dead bodies of the faithfull. For if he is permitted to enter in their liuing bodies, even when they are ioyned with the soule: how much more will God permit him to enter in their dead carions, which is no more man, but the filthie and corruptible caise of man. For as Christ sayth, It is not any thing that enters within man that defiles him, but onely that which proccedes and commeth out of him.[3]

3. Mark. 7.

CHAP. V.

ARGUMENT.

The description of the fourth kinde of Spirites called the Phairie: What is possible therein, and what is but illusiones. How far this Dialogue entreates of all these thinges, and to what end.

Philomathes. Now I pray you come on to that fourth kinde of spirites.

Epi. That fourth kinde of spirites, which by the Gentiles was called Diana, and her wandring court, and amongst us was called the Phairie (as I tould you) or our good neighboures, was one of the sortes of illusiones that was rifest in the time of Papistrie: for although it was holden odious to Prophesie by the devill, yet whome these kinde of Spirites carryed awaie, and informed, they were thought to be sonsiest and of best life. To speake of the many vaine trattles founded upon that illusion: How there was a King and Queene of Phairie, of such a iolly court & train as they had, how they had a teynd, & dutie, as it were, of all goods: how they naturallie rode and went, eate and drank, and did all other actiones like naturall men and women: I thinke it liker Virgils Campi Elysij, nor anie thing that ought to be beleeved by Christians, except in generall, that as I spake sundrie times before, the devil illuded the senses of sundry simple creatures, in making them beleeve that they saw and harde such thinges as were nothing so indeed.

Phi. But how can it be then, that sundrie Witches have gone to death with that confession, that they have ben transported with the Phairie to such a hill, which opening, they went in, and there saw a faire Queene, who being now lighter, gave them a stone that had sundrie vertues, which at sundrie times hath bene produced in judgement?

Epi. I say that, even as I said before of that imaginar rauishing of the spirite foorth of the bodie. For may not the devil object to their fantasie, their senses being dulled, and as it were a sleepe, such hilles & houses within them, such glistering courts and traines, and whatsoever such like wherewith he pleaseth to delude them. And in the meane time their bodies being senselesse, to convay in their hande any stone or such like thing, which he makes them to imagine to have received in such a place.

Phi. But what say ye to their fore-telling the death of sundrie persones, whome they alleage to have scene in these places? That is, a sooth-dreame (as they say) since they see it walking.

Epi. I thinke that either they have not bene sharply inough examined, that gave so blunt a reason for their Prophesie, or otherwaies, I thinke it likewise as possible that the Devill may prophesie to them when he deceives their imaginationes in that sorte, as well as when he plainely speakes unto them at other times for their prophesying, is but by a kinde of vision, as it were, wherein he commonly counterfeits God among the

Ethnicks, as I told you before.

Phi. I would know now whether these kindes of spirites may only appeare to Witches, or if they may also appeare to anie other.

Epi. They may do to both, to the innocent sort, either to affraie them, or to seeme to be a better sorte of folkes nor uncleane spirites are, and to the Witches, to be a cullour of safetie for them, that ignorant Magistrates may not punish them for it, as I told even now. But as the one sorte, for being perforce troubled with them ought to be pittied, so ought the other sorte (who may bee discerned by their taking uppon them to Prophesie by them,) That sorte I say, ought as severely to be punished as any other Witches, and rather the more, that that they goe dissemblingly to woorke.

Phi. And what makes the spirites have so different names from others.

Epi. Even the knaverie of that same devil; who as hee illudes the Necromancers with innumerable feyned names for him and his angels, as in special, making Sathan, Beelzebub, & Lucifer, to be three sundry spirites, where we finde the two former, but divers names given to the Prince of all the rebelling angels by the Scripture. As by Christ, the Prince of all the Devilles is called, Beelzebub in that place, which I alleaged against the power of any hereticques to cast out Devils. By John in the Revelation, the old tempter is called, Sathan the Prince of all the evill angels. And the last, to wit, Lucifer, is but by allegoric taken from the day Starre (so named in divers places of the Scriptures) because of his excellencie (I meane the Prince of them) in his creation before his fall. Even so I say he deceaves the Witches, by attributing to himselfe divers names: as if every divers shape that he trans formes himselfe in, were a divers kinde of spirit.

Phi. But I have hard many moe strange tales of this Phairie, nor ye have yet told me.

Epi. As well I do in that, as I did in all the rest of my discourse. For because the ground of this conference of ours, proceeded of your speering at me at our meeting, if there was such a thing as Witches or spirites: And if they had any power: I therefore have framed my whole discours, only to prove that such things are and may be, by such number of examples as I show to be possible by reason: & keepes me from dipping any further in playing the part of a Dictionarie, to tell what ever I have read or harde in that purpose, which both would exceede fayth, and rather would seeme to teach such unlawfull artes, nor to disallow and condemne them, as it is the duetie of all Christians to do.

CHAP. VI.

ARGUMENT.

Of the tryall and punishment of Witches. What sorte of accusation ought to be admitted against them. What is the cause of the increasing so far of their number in this age.

Philomathes. Then to make an ende of our conference, since I see it drawes late, what forme of punishment thinke ye merites these Magicians and Witches? For I see that ye account them to be all alike guiltie?

Epi. They ought to be put to death according to the Law of God, the civill and imperial law, and municipall law of all Christian nations.

Phi. But what kinde of death I pray you?

Epi. It is commonly used by fire, but that is an indifferent thing to be used in every cuntrie, according to the Law or custome thereof.

Phi. But ought no sexe, age nor ranck to be exempted?

Epi. None at al (being so used by the lawful Magistrate) for it is the highest poynt of Idolatrie, wherein no exception is admitted by the law of God.

Phi. Then bairnes may not be spared?

Epi. Yea, not a haire the lesse of my conclusion. For they are not that capable of reason as to practise such thinges. And for any being in company and not reveiling thereof, their lesse and ignorant age will no doubt excuse them.

Phi. I see ye condemne them all that are of the counsell of such craftes.

Epi. No doubt, for as I said, speaking of Magie, the consulters, trusters in, over-seers, interteiners or sturrers up of these craftes-folkes, are equallie guiltie with themselves that are the practisers.

Phi. Whether may the Prince then, or supreame Magistrate, spare or over-see any that are guiltie of that craft? upon som great respects knowen to him?

Epi. The Prince or Magistrate for further tryals cause, may continue the punishing of them such a certaine space as he thinkes convenient: But in the end to spare the life, and not to strike when God bids strike, and so severelie punish in so odious a fault & treason against God, it is not only unlawful, but doubtlesse no lesse sinne in that Magistrate, nor it was in Savles sparing of Agag. And so comparable to the sin of Witch-craft it selfe, as Samuell alleaged at that time.[1]

1. 1. Sam. 15.

Phi. Surely then, I think since this crime ought to be so severely punished. Judges ought to beware to condemne any, but such as they are sure are guiltie, neither should the clattering reporte of a carling serue in so weightie a case.

Epi. Iudges ought indeede to beware whome they condemne: For it is as great a crime (as Salomon sayeth,) To condemne the innocent, as to let the guiltie escape free;[2] neither ought the report of any one infamous person, be admitted for a sufficient proofe, which can stand of no law.

Phi. And what may a number then of guilty persons confessions, woork against one that is accused?

Epi. The assise must serue for interpretour of our law in that respect. But in my opinion, since in a mater of treason against the Prince, barnes or wives, or never so diffamed persons, may of our law serue for sufficient witnesses and proofes. I thinke surely that by a far greater reason, such witnesses may be sufficient in matters of high treason against God: For who but Witches can be prooves, and so witnesses of the doings of Witches.

Phi. Indeed, I trow they wil be loath to put any honest man upon their counsell. But what if they accuse folke to have bene present at their Imaginar conventiones in the spirite, when their bodies lyes sencelesse, as ye have said.

Epi. I think they are not a haire the lesse guiltie: For the Devill durst never have borrowed their shaddow or similitude to that turne, if their consent had not bene at it: And the consent in these turnes is death of the law.

2. Pro. 17.

Phi. Then Samuel was a Witch: For the Devill resembled his shape, and played his person in giuing response to Saule.

Epi. Samuel was dead aswell before that; and so none coulde slander him with medling in that unlawfull arte. For the cause why, as I take it, that God will not permit Sathan to use the shapes or similitudes of any innocent persones at such unlawful times, is that God wil not permit that any innocent persons shalbe slandered with that vile defection: for then the devil would find waies anew, to calumniate the best. And this we have in proofe by them that are carryed with the Phairie, who never see the shaddowes of any in that courte, but of them that thereafter are tryed to have bene brethren and sisters of that craft. And this was likewise proved by the confession of a young Lasse, troubled with spirites, laide on her by Witchcraft. That although shee saw the shapes of diverse men & women troubling her, and naming the persons whom these shaddowes represents: yet never one of them are found to be innocent, but al clearely tried to be most guilty, & the most part of them confessing the same. And besides that, I think it hath ben seldome harde tell of, that any whome persones guiltie of that crime accused, as having knowen them to be their marrowes by eye-sight, and not by hear-say, but such as were so accused of Witch-craft, could not be clearely tryed upon them, were at the least publickly knowen to be of a very euil life & reputation: so iealous is God I say, of the fame of them that are innocent in such causes. And besides that; there are two other good helpes that may be used for their trial: the one is the finding of their marke, and the trying the insensiblenes thereof. The other is their fleeting on the water: for as in a secret murther, if the deade carcase be at any time thereafter handled by the murtherer, it wil gush out of bloud, as if the blud wer crying to the Heaven for revenge of the murtherer, God having appoynted that secret super-naturall signe, for tryall of that secrete unnaturall crime, so it appeares that God hath appoynted (for a super-naturall signe of the monstruous impietie of the Witches) that the water shal refuse to receive them in her bosom, that have shaken off them the sacred Water of Baptisme, and wilfullie refused the benefite thereof: No not so much as their eyes are able to shed teares (thretten and torture them as ye please) while first they repent (God not permitting them to dissemble their obstinacie in so horrible a crime) albeit the women kinde especially, be able other-waies to shed teares at every light occasion when they will, yea, although it were dissemblingly like the Crocodiles.

Phi. Well, wee made this conference to last as long as leasure would permit: And to conclude then, since I am to take my leave of you, I pray God to purge this Cuntrie of these divellishe practises: for they were never so rife in these partes, as they are now.

Epi. I pray God that so be to. But the causes ar over manifest, that makes them to be so rife. For the greate wickednesse of the people on the one parte, procures this horrible defection, whereby God justlie punisheth sinne, by a greater iniquitie. And on the other part, the consummation of the worlde, and our deliverance drawing neare, makes Sathan to rage the more in his instruments, knowing his kingdome to be so neare an ende. And so fare-well for this time.[3]

FINIS.

3. Revel. 12.

NEWES FROM SCOTLAND.

NEWES FROM SCOTLAND.

Declaring the Damnable life and death of Doctor Fian, a notable Sorcerer, who was burned at Edenbrough in January last. 1591.

Which Doctor was regester to the Divell that sundry times preached at North Barrick Kirke, to a number of notorious Witches.

With the true examinations of the saide Doctor and Witches, as they uttered them in the presence of the Scottish King.

Discovering how they pretended to bewitch and drowne his Maiestie in the Sea comming from Denmark with such other wonderfull matters as the like hath not been heard of at any time.

Published according to the Scottish Coppie.

AT LONDON

Printed for William Wright.

TO THE READER

TO THE READER.

To the Reader.

The Manifolde untruthes which is spread abroade, concerning the detestable actions and apprehension of those Witches wherof this Historye following truely entreateth, hath caused me to publish the same in print: and the rather for that sundrie written Copies are lately dispersed therof, containing, that the said witches were first discovered, by meanes of a poore Pedler trauailing to the towne of Trenent, and that by a wonderfull manner he was in a moment convayed at midnight, from Scotland to Burdeux in Fraunce (beeing places of no small distance between) into a Marchants Seller there, & after, being sent from Burdeux into Scotlandby certaine Scottish Marchants to the Kinges Maiestie, that he discovered those Witches and was the cause of their apprehension: with a number of matters miraculous and incredible: All which in truthe are moste false. Nevertheles to satisfie a number of honest mindes, who are desirous to be enformed of the veritie and trueth of their confessions, which for certaintie is more stranger then the common reporte runneth, and yet with more trueth I have undertaken to publish this short Treatise, which declareth the true discourse of all that hath hapned, & aswell what was pretended by those wicked and detestable Witches against the

Kinges Maiestie, as also by what meanes they wrought the same.

All which examinations (gentle Reader) I have heere truelye published, as they were taken and uttered in the presence of the Kings Maiestie, praying thee to accept it for veritie, the same beeing so true as cannot be reproved.

DISCOURSE

DISCOURSE.

A true discourse, of the apprehension of sundrye Witches lately taken in Scotland, some are executed, and some are yet imprisoned.

With a particuler recitall of their examinations, taken in the presence of the Kinges Maiestie.

God by his omnipotent power, hath at al times and daily doth take such care, and is so vigillant, for the weale and preseruation of his owne, that thereby he disapointeth the wicked practises and euil intents of all such as by any meanes whatsoever, seeke indirectly to conspire any thing contrary to his holy will: yea and by the same power, he hath lately overthrown and hindered the intentions and wicked dealinges of a great number of ungodly creatures, no better then Divels: who suffering themselves to be allured and inticed by the Divell whom they serued, and to whome they were privatelye sworne: entered into the detestable Art of witchcraft, which they studied and practised so long time, that in the end they had seduced by their sorcery a number of other to be as bad as themselves: dwelling in the boundes of Lowthian, which is a principall shire or parte of Scotland, where the Kings Maiestie useth to make his cheefest residence or abode: and to the end that their detestable wickednes which they privilye had pretended against the Kings Maiestie, the Common-weale of that Country, with the Nobilitie and subjects of the same, should come to light: God of his unspeakeable goodnes did reveale and lay it open in very strange sorte, therby to make knowne unto the worlde, that there actions were contrarye to the lawe of God, and the naturall affection which we ought generallye to beare one to another: the manner of the revealing wherof was as followeth.

Within the towne of Trenent in the Kingdome of Scotland, there dwelleth one Dauid Seaton, who being deputie Bailiffe in the saide Towne, had a maide seruant called Geillis Duncane, who used secretly to be absent and to lye foorth of her Maisters house every other night: this Geillis Duncane took in hand to help all such as were troubled or greeved with any kinde of sicknes or infirmitie: and in short space did perfourme manye matters most miraculous, which thinges forasmuch as she began to doe them upon a sodaine, having never doon the like before, made her Maister and others to be in great admiracion, and wondred thereat: by meanes wherof the saide Dauid Seaton had his maide in some great suspition, that she did not those things by naturall and lawfull wayes, but rather supposed it to be doone by some extraordinary and unlawfull meanes.

Wherupon, her Maister began to growe very inquisitive, and examined her which way and by what meanes she were able to perfourme matters of so great importance: whereat she gave him no answere, neverthelesse, her Maister to the intent that he might the better trye and finde out the trueth of the same, did with the helpe of others, torment her with the torture of the Pilliwinckes upon her fingers, which is a greeuous torture, and binding or wrinching her head with a corde or roape, which is a most cruell torment also, yet would she not confesse any thing, whereupon they suspecting that she had beene marked by the Divell (as commonly witches are) made dilligent search about her, and found the enemies marke to be in her fore crag or foreparte of her throate: which being found, she confessed that all her dooings was doone by the wicked allurements and inticements of the Divell, and that she did them by witchcraft.

After this her confession, she was committed to prison, where she continued for a season, where immediatly she accused these persons following to be notorious witches, and caused them foorthwith to be apprehended one after an other, vidz. Agnis Sampson the eldest Witch of them al, dwelling in Haddington, Agnes Tompson of Edenbrough, Doctor Fian, alias John Cunningham, maister of the Schoole at Saltpans in Lowthian, of whose life and strange actes, you shall heare more largely in the ende of this discourse: these were by the saide Geillis Duncane accused, as also George Motts wife dwelling in Saltpans, Robert Griersonnskipper, and Iennit Bandilandis, with the Porters wife of Seaton, the Smith at the brigge Hallis with innumerable others in that partes, and dwelling in those bounds aforesaide: of whom some are alreadye executed, the rest remaine in prison, to receive the doome of Iudgement at the Kings maiesties will and pleasure.

The said Geillis Duncane also caused Ewphame Meealrean to be apprehended, who conspired and perfourmed the death of her Godfather, and who used her art upon a gentleman being one of the Lords and Iustices of the Session, for bearing good will to her Daughter: she also caused to be apprehended one Barbara Naper, for bewitching to death Archibalde, last Earle of Angus, who languished to death by witchcraft and yet the same was not suspected, but that he died of so strange a disease, as the Phisition knew not how to cure or remedy the same: but of all other the saide witches, these two last before recited, were reputed for as civill honest women as any that dwelled within the Citie of Edenbrough, before they were apprehended. Many other besides were taken dwelling in Lieth, who are detayned in prison, untill his Maiesties further will and pleasure be known:

of whose wicked dooings you shall particularly heare, which was as followeth.

This aforeaside Agnis Sampson which was the elder Witch, was taken and brought to Haliciud house before the Kings Maiestie and sundry other of the nobility of Scotland, where she was straitly examined, but all the perswasions which the Kings maiestie used to her with the rest of his counsell, might not prouoke or induce her to confesse any thing, but stood stiffely in the deniall of all that was laide to her charge: wherupon they caused her to be conveied awaye to prison, there to receive such torture as hath been lately prouided for witches in that country: and forasmuch as by due examination of witchcraft and witches in Scotland, it hath latelye beene found that the Devill dooth generallye marke them with a privie marke, by reason the Witches have confessed themselves, that the Divell dooth lick them with his tung in some privy part of their bodie, before hee dooth receive them to be his seruants, which marke commonly is given them under the haire in some part of their bodye, wherby it may not easily be found out or scene, although they be searched: and generally so long as the marke is not seene to those which search them, so long the parties that hath the marke will never confesse any thing. Therfore by special commaundement this Agnis Sampson had all her haire sn of, in each parte of her bodie, and her head thrawen with a rope according to the custome of that Countrye, beeing a paine most greeuous, which she continued almost an hower, during which time she would not confesse any thing untill the Divels marke was found upon her privities, then she immediatlye confessed whatsoever was demaunded of her, and iustifying those persons aforesaid to be notorious witches.

Item, the saide Agnis Tompson was after brought againe before the Kings Maiestie and his Counsell, and being examined of the meetings and detestable dealings of those witches, she confessed that upon the night of Allhollon Even last, she was accompanied aswell with the persons aforesaide, as also with a great many other witches, to the number of two hundreth: and that all they together went by Sea each one in a Riddle or Cive, and went in the same very substantially with Flaggons of wine making merrie and drinking by the waye in the same Riddles or Cives, to the Kerke of North Barrick in Lowthian, and that after they had landed, tooke handes on the land and daunced this reill or short daunce, singing all with one voice.

Commer goe ye before, commer goe ye,
If ye will not goe before, commer let me.

At which time she confessed, that this Geilles Duncane did goe before them playing this reill or daunce upon a small Trump, called a Jewes Trump, untill they entred into the Kerk of north Barrick.

These confessions made the King in a woderful admiration, and sent for the said Geillis Duncane, who upon the like Trump did playe the said daunce before the Kings Maiestie, who in respect of the strangenes of these matters, tooke great delight to bee present at their examinations.

Item, the said Agnis Tompson confessed that the Divell being then at North Barrick Kerke attending their comming in the habit or likenes of a man, and seeing that they tarried over long, he at their comming enioyned them all to a pennance, which was, that they should kisse his Buttockes, in signe of duetye to him: which being put over the Pulpit barre, everye one did as he had enioyned them: and having made his ungodly exhortations, wherein he did greatlye enveighe against the King of Scotland, he received their oathes for their good and true service towards him, and departed: which doone, they returned to Sea, and so home againe.

At which time the witches demaunded of the Divel why he did beare such hatred to the King, who answered, by reason the King is the greatest enemy he hath in the worlde: all which their confessions and depositions are still extant upon record.

Item, the saide Agnis Sampson confessed before the Kings Maiestie sundrye thinges which were so miraculous and strange, as that his Maiestie saide they were all extreame lyars, wherat she answered, she would not wishe his Maiestie to suppose her woords to be false, but rather to beleeve them, in that she would discover such matter unto him as his maiestie should not any way doubt off.

And therupon taking his Maiestie a little aside, she declared unto him the verye woordes which passed betweene the Kings Maiestie and his Queene at Upslo in Norway the first night of their mariage, with their answere eache to other: whereat the Kinges Maiestie wondered greatlye, and swore by the liuing God, that he beleeved that all the Divels in hell could not have discovered the same: acknowledging her woords to be most true, and therefore gave the more credit to the rest which is before declared.

Touching this Agnis Tompson, she is the onlye woman, who by the Divels perswasion should have entended and put in execution the Kings Maiesties death in this manner.

She confessed that she tooke a blacke Toade, and did hang the same up by the heeles, three daies, and collected and gathered the venome as it dropped and fell from it in an Oister shell, and kept the same venome close covered, untill she should obtaine any parte or peece of foule linnen cloth, that had appertained to the Kings Maiestie, as shirt, handkercher, napkin or any other thing which she practised to obtaine by meanes of one John Kers, who being attendant in his Maiesties Chamber, desired him for olde acquaintance betweene them, to helpe her to one or a peece of such a cloth as is aforesaide, which thing the said John Kers denyed to helpe her too, saying he could not help her too it.

And the said Agnis Tompson by her depositions since her apprehension saith, that if she had obtained any one peece of linnen cloth which the King had worne and fouled, she had bewitched him to death, and put him to such extraordinary paines, as if he had beene lying upon sharp thornes and endes of Needles.

Moreover she confessed that at the time when his Maiestie was in Denmarke, she being accompanied with the parties before specially named, tooke a Cat and christened it, and afterward bound to each parte of that Cat, the cheefest partes of a dead man, and severall ioynts of his bodie, and that in the night following the saide Cat was conveied into the midst of the sea by all these witches sayling in their riddles or Cives as is aforesaide, and so left the saide Cat right before the Towne of Lieth in Scotland: this doone, there did arise such a tempest in the Sea, as a greater hath not beene seene: which tempest was the cause of the perrishing of a Boate or vessell comming over from the towne of Brunt Iland to the towne of Lieth, wherein was sundrye Jewelles and riche giftes, which should have been presented to the now Queen of Scotland, at her Maiesties comming to Lieth.

Againe it is confessed, that the said christened Cat was the cause that the Kinges Maiesties Ship at his comming foorth of Denmarke, had a contrary winde to the rest of his Ships, then being in his companye, which thing was most strange and true, as the Kings Maiestie acknowledgeth, for when the rest of the Shippes had a faire and good winde, then was the winde contrarye and altogither against his Maiestie: and further the saide witche declared, that his Maiestie had never come safelye from the Sea, if his faith had not prevailed aboue their ententions.

Moreover the said Witches being demaunded how the Divell would use them when he was in their company, they confessed that when the Divell did receive them for his seruants, and that they had vowed themselves unto him, then he would Carnallye use them, albeit to their little pleasure, in respect of his colde nature: and would doo the like at sundry other times.

As touching the aforesaide Doctor Fian, alias John Cunningham, the examination of his actes since his apprehension, declareth the great subtiltye of the divell, and therfore maketh thinges to appeere the more miraculous: for being apprehended by the accusation of the saide Geillis Duncane aforesaide, who confessed he was their Regester, and that there was not one man suffered to come to the Divels readinges but onlye he: the saide Doctor was taken and imprisoned, and used with the accustomed paine, prouided for those offences, inflicted upon the rest as is aforesaide.

First by thrawing of his head with a roape, wherat he would confesse nothing.

Secondly, he was perswaded by faire means to confesse his follies, but that would prevaile as little.

Lastly he was put to the most severe and cruell paine in the world, called the bootes, who after he had received three strokes, being enquired if he would confesse his damnable acts and wicked life, his tung would not serue him to speak, in respect wherof the rest of the witches willed to search his tung, under which was found two pinnes thrust up into the head, whereupon the witches did laye, Now is the Charme stinted, and shewed that those charmed Pinnes were the cause he could not confesse any thing: then was he immediatly released of the bootes, brought before the King, his confession was taken, and his owne hand willingly set ther-unto, which contained as followeth.

First, that at the generall meetinges of those witches, hee was alwayes preasent: that he was Clarke to all those that were in subiection to the Divels service, bearing the name of witches, that alwaye he did take their othes for their true service to the Divell, and that he wrot for them such matters as the Divell still pleased to commaund him.

Item, he confessed that by his witchcrafte he did bewitch a Gentleman dwelling neere to the Saltpans, where the said Doctor kept Schoole, onely for being enamoured of a Gentlewoman whome he loued himselfe: by meanes of which his Sorcerye, witchcraft and divelish practises, he caused the said Gentleman that once in xxiiij. howres he fell into a lunacie and madnes, and so continued one whole hower together, and for the veritie of the same, he caused the Gentleman to be brought before the Kinges Maiestie, which was upon the xxiiij. day of December last, and being in his Maiesties Chamber, suddenly he gave a great scritch and fell into a madnes, sometime bending himselfe, and sometime capring so directly up, that his head did touch the seeling of the Chamber, to the great admiration of his Maiestie and others then present: so that all the Gentlemen in the Chamber were not able to holde him, untill they called in more helpe, who together bound him hand and foot: and suffering the said gentleman to lye still untill his furye were past, he within an hower came againe to himselfe, when being demaunded of the Kings Maiestie what he saw or did all that while, answered that he had been in a sound sleepe.

Item the said Doctor did also confesse that he had used means sundry times to obtain his purpose and wicked intent of the same Gentlewoman, and seeing himselfe disapointed of his intention, he determined by all waies he might to obtaine the same, trusting by coniuring, witchcraft and Sorcery to obtaine it in this manner.

It happened this gentlewoman being unmaried, had a brother who went to schoole with the said Doctor, and calling his Scholler to him, demaunded if he did lye with his sister, who answered he did, by meanes wherof he thought to obtaine his purpose, and therefore secretlye promised to teach him without stripes, so he would obtain for him three haires of his sisters privities, at such time as he should spye best occasion for it: which the youth promised faithfullye to perfourme, and vowed speedily to put it in practise, taking a peece of coniured paper of his maister to lappe them in when he had gotten them: and thereupon the boye practised nightlye to obtaine his maisters purpose, especially when his sister was a sleepe.

But God who knoweth the secrets of all harts, and revealeth all wicked and ungodlye practises, would not suffer the intents of this divilish Doctor to come to that purpose which he supposed it would, and therefore to declare that he was heauilye offended with his wicked entent, did so woorke by the Gentlewomans owne meanes, that in the ende the same was discovered and brought to light: for she being one night a sleepe, and her brother in bed with her, suddenlye cryed out to her mother, declaring that her Brother would not suffer her to sleepe, whereupon her mother having a quick capacitie, did vehemently suspect Doctor Fiansentention, by reason she was a witche of her selfe, and therefore presently arose, and was very inquisitive of the boy to understand his intent, and the better to know the same, did beat him with sundry stripes, wherby he discovered the trueth unto her.

The Mother therefore being well practised in witchcrafte, did thinke it most convenient to meete with the Doctor in his owne Arte, and thereupon tooke the paper from the boy, wherein hee should have put the same haires, and went to a young Heyfer which never had borne Calfe nor gone to the Bull, and with a paire of sheeres, clipped off three haires from the vdder of the Cow, and wrapt them in the same paper, which she againe delivered to the boy, then willing him to give the same to his saide Maister, which he immediatly did.

The Schoolemaister so soone as he had received them,

thinking them indeede to bee the Maides haires, went straight and wrought his arte upon them: But the Doctor had no sooner doone his intent to them, but presentlye the Hayfer or Cow whose haires they were indeed, came unto the doore of the Church wherein the Schoolemaister was, into the which the Hayfer went, and made towards the Schoolemaister, leaping and dauncing upon him, and following him foorth of the church and to what place so ever he went, to the great admiration of all the townes men of Saltpans, and many other who did beholde the same.

The reporte whereof made all men imagine that hee did woorke it by the Divell, without whom it could never have beene so sufficientlye effected: and therupon, the name of the said Doctor Fian (who was but a very yong man) began to grow so common among the people of Scotland, that he was secretlye nominated for a notable Cuniurer.

All which although in the beginning he denied, and would not confesse, yet having felt the pain of the bootes (and the charme stinted, as aforesayd) he confessed all the aforesaid to be most true, without producing anie witnesses to iustifie the same, & therupon before the kings maiesty he subscribed the sayd confessions with his owne hande, which for truth remaineth upon record in Scotland.

After that the depositions and examinations of the sayd doctor Fian Alias Cuningham was taken, as alreadie is declared, with his owne hand willingly set thereunto, hee was by the master of the prison committed to ward, and appointed to a chamber by himselfe, where forsaking his wicked wayes, acknowledging his most ungodly lyfe, shewing that he had too much folowed the allurements and entisements of Sathan, and fondly practised his conclusions by coniuring, witchcraft, inchantment, sorcerie, and such like, hee renounced the devill and all his wicked workes, vowed to leade the life of a Christian, and seemed newly connected towards God.

The morrow after upon conference had with him, he granted that the devill had appeared unto him in the night before, appareled all in blacke, with a white wand in his hande, and that the devill demaunded of him if hee would continue his faithfull service, according to his first oath and promise made to that effect. Whome (as hee then sayd) he utterly renounced to his face, and sayde unto him in this manner, Avoide Satan, avoide, for I have listned too much unto thee, and by the same thou hast undone mee, in respect whereof I utterly forsake thee. To whome the devill answered, That once ere thou die thou shall bee mine. And with that (as he sayde) the devill brake the white wande, and immediatly vanished foorth of his sight

Thus all the daie this Doctor Fian continued verie solitarie, and seemed to have care of his owne soule, and would call uppon God, shewing himselfe penitent for his wicked life, neverthelesse the same night hee founde such meanes, that hee stole the key of the prison doore and chamber in the which he was, which in the night hee opened and fled awaie to the Salt pans, where hee was alwayes resident, and first apprehended. Of whose sodaine departure when the Kings maiestie had intelligence, hee presently commanded diligent inquirie to bee made for his apprehension, and for the better effecting thereof, hee sent publike proclamations into all partes of his lande to the same effect. By meanes of whose hot and harde pursuite, he was agayn taken and brought to prison, and then being called before the kings highnes, hee was reexamined as well touching his departure, as also touching all that had before happened.

But this Doctor, notwithstanding that his owne confession appeareth remaining in recorde under his owne hande writing, and the same thereunto fixed in the presence of the Kings maiestie and sundrie of his Councell, yet did hee utterly denie the same.

Whereupon the kinges maiestie perceiving his stubbourne wilfulnesse, concerned and imagined that in the time of his absence hee had entered into newe conference and league with the devill his master, and that hee had beene agayne newly marked, for the which hee was narrowly searched, but it coulde not in anie wise bee founde, yet for more tryall of him to make him confesse, hee was commaunded to have a most straunge torment which was done in this manner following.

His nailes upon all his fingers were riven and pulled off with an instrument called in Scottish a Turkas, which in England wee call a payre of pincers, and under everie nayle there was thrust in two needels over even up to the heads. At all which tormentes notwithstanding the Doctor never shronke anie whit, neither woulde he then confesse it the sooner for all the tortures inflicted upon him.

Then was hee with all convenient speed, by commandement, convaied againe to the torment of the bootes, wherein hee continued a long time, and did abide so many blowes in them, that his legges were crushte and beaten togeather as small as might bee, and the bones and flesh so brused, that the bloud and marrowe spouted forth in great abundance, whereby they were made unserviceable for ever. And notwithstanding al these grieuous paines and cruell torments hee would not confesse anie thing, so deepely had the devill entered into his heart, that hee utterly denied all that which he had before auouched, and woulde saie nothing thereunto but this, that what hee had done and sayde before, was onely done and sayde for feare of paynes which he had endured.

Upon great consideration therefore taken by the Kings maiestie and his Councell, as well for the due execution of iustice uppon such detestable malefactors, as also for example sake, to remayne a terrour to all others heereafter, that shall attempt to deale in the lyke wicked and ungodlye actions, as witchcraft, sorcery, cuniuration, & such lyke, the sayde Doctor Fian was soone after araigned, condemned, and adiudged by the law to die, and then to bee burned according to the lawe of that lande, prouided in that behalfe. Whereupon hee was put into a carte, and beeing first strangled, hee was immediatly put into a great fire, being readie prouided for that purpose, and there burned in the Castle hill of Edenbrough on a saterdaie in the ende of Januarie last past. 1591. The rest of the witches which are not yet executed, remayne in prison till farther triall, and knowledge of his maiesties pleasure.

This strange discourse before recited, may perhaps give some occasion of doubt to such as shall happen to reade the same, and thereby coniecture that the Kings maiestie would not hazarde himselfe in the presence of such notorious witches, least therby might have insued great danger to his person and the generall state of the land, which thing in truth might wel have bene feared. But to answer generally to such, let this suffice: that first it is well knowen that the King is the child & seruant of God, and they but seruants to the devil, hee is the Lords annointed, and they but vesselles of Gods wrath: he is a true Christian, and trusteth in God, they worse than Infidels, for they onely trust in the devill, who daily serue them, till he have brought them to utter destruction. But heereby it seemeth that his Highnesse carted a magnanimious and undanted mind, not feared with their inchantmentes, but resolute in this, that so long as God is with him, hee feareth not who is against him. And trulie the whole scope of this treatise dooth so plainely laie open the wonderfull prouidence of the Almightie, that if he had not bene defended by his omnipotencie and power, his Highnes had never returned alive in his voiage frõ Denmarke, so that there is no doult but God woulde as well defend him on the land as on the sea, where they pretended their damnable practise.

THE WITCHCRAFT ACT

1604

THE WITCHCRAFT ACT 1604

An Acte against Conjuration, Witchcrafte
and dealinge with evill and wicked Spirits.
1604: 1 James 1 c.12:

BE it enacted by the King our Soveraigne Lord; the Lords Spirituall and Temporall, and the Commons in this present Parliament assembled, and by the authority of the same, that the Statute made in the fifth yeare of the Reigne of our late Soveraigne Lady of most Famous and Happy memory, Queen Elizabeth, Entituled, An Acte againste Conjurations, Inchantments and Witchcraftes; be from the Feast of Saint Michael the Archangel next coming, for and concerning all offences to bee committed after the same Feaste, utterly repealed.[1]

And for the better restraining of said offences, and more severe punishing the same, be it further Enacted by the Authority aforesaid; That if any person or persons, after the said Feast of St. Michael the Archangell next coming, shall use, practise, or exercise any invocation or conjuration of any evil and wicked spirit: or shall consult, covenant with, entertaine, imploy, feed, or reward any evil and wicked spirit, to or for any intent or

1. (Eliz. c. 16. repealed)

purpose; or take up any dead man, woman, or child, out of his, her, or their grave, or any other place where the dead body resteth; or the skin, bone, or any other part of any dead person, to be imployed, or used in any manner of Witchcraft, Sorcery, Charme, or Inchantment, or shall use, practise, or exercise, any Witchcraft, Incantment, Charme or Sorcery, whereby any person shall be Killed, Destroyed, Wasted, Consumed, Pined, or Lamed, in His or Her body, or any part therof; that then every such Offender, or Offenders, their Ayders, Abettors, and Counsellors, being of the said offences duly and lawfully Convicted and Attainted, shall suffer paines of death as a Felon or Felons, and shall lose the priviledge and benefit of Clergy and Sanctuary.[2]

And further, to the intent that all manner of practise, use or exercise of Witchcraft, Inchantment, Charme, or Sorcery, should be from henceforth utterly avoided, abolished, and taken away: Be it Enacted by the Authority of this present Parliament, that if any person or persons, shall from and after the said Feast of Saint Michaell the Archangell next coming, take upon him or them, by Witchcraft, Inchantment, Charme, or Sorcery, to tell or declare in what place any Treasure of Golde or Silver should or might be found or had in the earth, or other secret places; or where goods, or things lost, or stolne, should be found or become, or to the intent to provoke any person to unlawfull love, or whereby any Cattell, or Goods of any person shall be destroyed, wasted, or impaired; or to hurt or destroy any person in his or her body, although the same be not effected and done, that then all and every such person or persons so offending, and being therof lawfully convicted,

2. Invoking or consulting with Evil Spirits, taking up Dead Bodies, &c. for the purposes of Witchcraft, &c. or practising Witchcraft, &c. to the Harm of others, declared Felony without Clergy..

shall for the said offence suffer imprisonment by the space of one whole year, without baile or maineprise; and once in every quarter of the said year, shall in some Market-Town, upon the Market day, or at such time as any faire shall be kept there, stand openly upon the Pillory by the space of six hours, and there shall openly confesse his or her errour and offence.[3]

And if any person or persons, being once convicted of the same offences as is aforesaid, do eftsoones perpetrate and commit the like offence, that then every such offender, being of any the said offences the second time lawfully, and duly convicted, and attainted as is aforesaid, shall suffer paines of death as a Felon, or Felons, and shall lose the benefit and priviledge of Clergy, and Sanctuary, saving to the wife of such person as shall offend in any thing contrary to this Act, her title of Dower, and also to the Heire and Successor of every such person, his, or their titles of inheritance, succession, and other rights, as though no such attainder of the Ancestor or Predecessor had been made: provided alwayes, that if the offender in any the cases aforesaid, shall happen to be a Peer of this Realm, then his tryall therein, to be had by his Peers, as it is used in cases of Felony or Treason, and not otherwise.

3. Penalty on declaring by Witchcraft where Treasure, &c. is hidden; procuring unawful Love; or attempting to hurt Cattle or Persons: 1st Offence Imprisonment; 2nd felony without Clergy.

SELECT
Cases of Conscience
TOUCHING
VVitches and VVitchcrafts.

By IOHN GAVLE, Preacher of the Word at Great *Staughton* in the County of *Huntington*.

Deut. 18. 10, 11, 12.

There shall not be found among you any one that maketh his Son or his Daughter to passe through the fire, or that useth Divination, or an observer of Times, or an Enchanter, or a Witch.

Or a Charmer, or a Consulter with familiar Spirits, or a Wizard, or a Necromancer.

For all that do these things are an Abomination unto the Lord: and because of these Abominations, the Lord thy God doth drive them out from before thee.

London, Printed by *W. Wilson* for *Richard Clutterbuck*, and are to be sold at his House in *Noblestreet*. 1646.

SELECT
CASES OF CONSCIENCE
TOUCHING
WITCHES AND WITCHCRAFTS.

By JOHN GAULE, Preacher
of the Word at Great Staughton
in the County of Huntington.

Deut. 18. 10, 11, 12.

*There shall not be found among you any one that maketh his
Son or his Daughter to passe through the fire, or that useth
Divination, or an observer of Times,
or an Enchanter, or a Witch.*

*Or a Charmer, or a Consulter with familiar Spirits, or a
Wizard, or a Necromancer.*

*For all that do these things are an Abomination unto the Lord:
and because of these Abominations, the Lord thy God doth drive
them out from before thee.*

London, Printed by W. Wilson for Richard Clutterbuck, and
are to be sold at his House in Noblestreet. 1646.
(1646)

I Have with much satisfaction and content perused this learned & judicious discourse, intituled Select Cases of Conscience concerning Witches and Witchcrafts. And finding it to bee very solide and seasonable, I allow it to bee Printed and published.

JOHN DOWNAME.

To his ever honoured Valentine Wauton Esquire, Colonell, and one of the Honorable House of Commons. As also to the other worthy Gentlemen; together with all the good people of the Parish of Great Staughton in the County of Huntington.

SIR,

YOU heresee, what the the rest of the Parish heard; under one moneths occasionall paines in my place. I am forced to make it publique, partly because I suffered some opposition & affront in my preaching, from one I never saw before; and partly because some opinions of it are spread since, by and among those that know me not. But chiefely to answer the expectation of those amongst whom I am knowne. I hope (what I here tender you) will speake the Trueth of an honest Conscience to the World; the Affection of a carefull Pastor to the rest; and to you Sir! the gratefull (because much ingaged) mind of

Your humble Servant, JOHN GAULE.

To the Judicious Reader.

Reader! I present thee here with a Letter; on occasion of this publishing. It were but lost labour to glosse upon it. Thou mayest easily, reade him, in his Letter, and mee, in my Booke.

M. N.

MY service to your Worship presented, I have this day received a Letter, &c.—to come to a Towne called Great Staughton to search for evill disposed persons called Witches (though I heare your Minister is farre against us through ignorance) I intend to come (God willing) the sooner to heare his singular Judgment on the behalfe of such parties; I have known a Minister in Suffolke preach as much against their discovery in a Pulpit, and forc'd to recant it (by the Committee) in the same place. I much marvaile such evill Members should have any (much more any of the Clergy) who should daily preach Terrour to convince such Offenders, stand up to take their parts against such as are Complainants for the King, and sufferers themselves with their Families and Estates. I intend to give your Towne a Visite suddenly, I am to come to Kimbolton this weeke, and it shall bee tenne to one but I will come to your Town first, but I would certainely know afore whether your Town affords many Sticklers for such Cattell, or willing to give and afford us good welcome and entertainement, as other where I have beene, else I shall wave your Shire (not as yet beginning in any part of it my selfe) And betake me to such places where I doe and may persist without controle, but with thankes and recompence So I humbly take my leave and rest,

Your Servant to be commanded,
Matthew Hopkins.

I

WHETHER IT OUGHT TO BE BELEEVED, THAT THERE ARE ANY WITCHES?

Hee that will needs perswade himself that there are no Witches, would as faine be perswaded, that there is no Devill; and hee that can already beleeve that there is no Devill, will ere long beleeve that there is no God. For there are much what the same grounds or motives both for the Atheist, and the Adiabolist. Both are errours and evills issuing, not only from a fond presuming folly, but also from a carnall dispensing security. Psal. 14. 1. And therefore when I consider that opinion of the Sadduces, Acts 23. 8. I cannot but wonder at the received ground for it. Who are said to deny all there cited, onely for this end; that so they might serve God more sincerely, and for himselfes sake; blessing him even for a present beeing; and not doing his wil, out of any expepectation of a future reward. Whereas our late leaners and lingerers after such a kinde of sect, could be content to deny all these, meerly for this intent that so they might serve themselves wholly, sin more greedily, live now more securely, and feare no future penalty. But as doating sleepes or dreams, awaken to greater distractions: so doe false opinions, to the more fearfull Convictions; Especially all fond perswasions touching God or the Divel (if not otherwise recanted) are confuted by their own sad experience at the last. And (as to the point in hand) I could instance from Story (but that I resolve against all such dilatations in this Epitome) how many have had no faith of witches being, til they have had a sense of them, and then their bewitched body or goods, has served to unbewitch them of their opinion & Conceit. But there are also a sect or sort, that (on the other hand) are as superstitious in this point, as these can be infidelious. They conclude peremptorily (not from reason, but indiscretion) that witches not only are, but are in every place, and Parish with them, every old woman with a wrinkled face, a furr'd brow, a hairy lip, a gobber tooth, a squint eye, a squeaking voyce, or a scolding tongue, having a rugged coate on her back, a skullcap on her head, a spindle in her hand, and a Dog or Cat by her side; is not only suspected, but pronounced for a witch. Every new disease, notable accident, mirable of nature, rarity of art, nay and strange work or just judgment of God; is by them accounted for no other, but an act or effect of witchcraft. And for this the Witch must bee suspected; and this suspition, though it bee but late, of a few, and those the under sort, yet is it enough to send for the Witch-searchers, or witch-seekers (a trade never taken up in England till this) whose lucratory skil and Experience is not much improved above the outward senses. For if you will not admit a big, or a boyl; a wart, or a wen; a push, or a pile; a scar, or a scabbe; an issue, or an ulcer; for a palpable Witches marke: yet then shall it certainly be determined to be in such a place, as for shame, and in very truth, is not to be named. Put to save the trouble and Charges of the witch-finder, they will undertake to try the Witch of themselves, yet by no other rules then those traditionall, and of their own superstition. Nay and (I tremble to record it) they will have the witch presently punished, and the issue thereof shall prove no lesse then capitall; and yet by no Law, but that of their own Lawlesse fury. Now of these two sorts, I hold the last not only the more numerous, but the more dangerous of the two. Not that I thinke there is charity in the one opinion, as I am sure there is iniquity in the other. But for as much as the superstition of the one, is one maine cause of the others Infidelity. For I have known the simpler meaning therefore backeward to beleeve any are thus guilty; while they have observed the ruder conditioned so overforward to pronounce upon the innocent: yea and some wise men too, have put it to a great dispute, because they have read (as appears in story) that men of the most eminent wisdome and holinesse of their times have (by such people as these) been slandered for Witches. I could give instance in Abraham, Joseph, Moses, Daniel, Athanasius, Wicklef, Luther, &c. And it is the more easie to be believed, in that our Saviour Christ himselfe, not only escaped not so blasphemous a Calumny, Matt. 9. 34. and 12. 24. (I abhor to speake what like Imputation of some in after Ages) but also foretold that his chiefest servants should bee slaundered in like manner, Mat. 10. 25. But what? did Christ therefore deny that there were any Witches? nay hee rather confesses it for distinction sake, Matt. 12. 27, 28. And verily no abuse of men (either on one side or other) must debarre from concluding of Truth. I therfore (in a plain and full way) determine here, as doe the orthodox, viz.

That as there have been; so ther are, & wil be witches unto the worlds end. When Witches first were in the world, is uncertain, before Pharaohs Magitians; we read Joseph talking (like an Aegyptian) of divination, Gen. 44. 5. 15. (which he spake certainly not to bewray his Profession, but conceal his Person.) Old Authors relate that Cham was the first Witch (who among the Gentiles was called Zoroaster) and that hee taught this divellish Art to his son Mizraim, and he to the Aegyptians his People; and they that their learning to the world. Some say, the Divell was the first Witch when hee plaid the Impostor with our first Parents, possessing the Serpent (as his Impe) to their delusion, Gen. 3. and it is whispered that our Grandame Eve was a little guilty of such a kind of Society, inasmuch as such an Enmity was immediately denounced upon it. But no matter whether Witches & Witchcrafts began with the world or no; we are too sure they are not like to end, but with the world, 1 Tim. 4. 1. And speaking of the world & Witches, I take roome enough to determine their Existence. For haply in some Places, and at some purer Times of the Church, a Witch may not then and there be found, Deut. 18. 10. Micah 5. 12. Zach. 13. 2. at least wise comparatively, not in those Multitudes, or Multiplicities. And thus explained my determination stands firm to any mans beliefe for these Reasons following.

1. Because the holy Scriptures speake of Witch-craft as of a specifique sin, 1 Sam. 15. 23. Gal. 5. 20. Now no accident can subsist without a Position or Concession of its proper subject in whom it must of necessity inhere. 2. The word of God discovers and describes them by their severall names, Deut. 18. 10. Now names are not given to things that are not: nay the variety of names serve to note their Multitude in the Concrete, as well as their multiplicity in the Abstract. 3. God Almighty has Enacted Lawes and Penalties against them, Exo. 22. 18. Lev. 20. 27. which were not instituted for, nor can be executed upon shadowes & meer nothing. 4. It is carefully forbidden to seeke after such, Levit. 19. 31. which how vaine were it if none such were to be found? Because though individuall acts may perish with the Authors, yet never any specifique sin (once here) quite vanished hence; but (through the common roote of Corruption) was propagated to all Ages. 6. Because the Devill (through his depraved knowledge) hath devised perpetuall Rules of Witch-crafts; such as he not only suggests immediately and

occasionally; but hath delivered them to impious wretches, to be traditionally taught and communicated from one Generation to another. 7. Because the Divell labours continually to uphold the visibility and eminency of his kingdome, which he doth in and by, none more then such as these. 8. Even Heathen by the light of Nature, have asserted such to be: nay and by the Law of Nature, convinced them to be such. 9. The opinion and judgement of so many learned men in all professions. (Philosophers, Historians, Lawyers, Physitians, Divines, Schoolmen, Summists, Casuists, Kings and Princes) that have shown so much Art and industry, in their demonstration and discovery. 10. The observation, Tradition, confession, practise and experiment hereof (in all Ages, and among all Nations) is more then manifest.

The Generall thus confirmed, let me also adde a touch upon these particulars. 1. That Witches have been more frequent in some Ages of the World, then others, namely, the more blind, dissolute, paganish, Idolatrous, superstitious. 2. That Witches have always abounded in some coasts of the World, more then others; as namely, where the Gospell is not; where it is not so plain, pure, and powerfull; and where Witch-craft is made either their Religion, or their Trade. 3. That Witches are to be found in some Religions, more then others, that is to say, not only wher witchcraft it selfe is counted a Religion; but where Religion it selfe is superstitious, and so disposing to Witch-craft. 4. That there has been, are, and are likely still to bee, more Witches under the Popish; then in the Protestant Religion. For not only their Popes, Priests, Fryers, Nuns, (many of them) have been notorious Witches: but their praestigious miracles, & superstitious rites little better then kindes of Witch-crafts.

Now though I find it easier to determine of Witches, that they are; then to discover what they are, yet I may give occasion to apprehend something to that purpose, from this one maine conclusion, viz. That Witch-craft, or the sin of Witches, is the most great & grievous, the most deadly & damnable sin, that a mortall man may be guilty of. I conceive it second to none that can possibly here be committed, and my Reasons are,

1. Because it is called an abomination unto the Lord, Deut. 18. 12. which is never said but of those Impieties that are of all other most Execrable.

2. Because all other sins and disobediences, are but compared to this for hainousnesse, 1 Sam. 15. 23. Now the thing compared is alwaies inferiour to that to which it is compared.

3. Because Witch-craft in Hebrew, Greek, and Latine is commonly called by the name of Evill-doing: signifying (as say the Antients) that it is the greatest evill that can be done.

4. Because it is the most malicious and immediate aversion from the greatest Good; and the most malicious and immediate conversion to the greatest Evill. For here is God Renounced and defied; and the Divell embraced and adored.

5. Because no sin upon earth so tempts God, as Witch-craft doth. Next to the Divells impudent tempting of Christ: was Balaams importunate tempting of God. It even tempts the Divell to tempt God. For little or nothing can the Divell doe for the Witch by a Leaguer Commission; but as hee is faine to tempt Gods Permission at every turn. Else Satan had not craved a second power against Job; after a confession of the first.

6. Because it is the most abhorred of all those sins, which we cal the sins against Nature. Not onely in regard of that horrid illusion of an Incubus: but also in respect of common society;

for as it is most naturall for man to be sociable, so it is most unnaturall to him to associate himselfe contrary to his kinde. And so much the more in this, in that it is against not only a naturally arising, but a divinely imposed Antipathy, Gen. 3. 15. 1 Cor. 10. 20.

7. Because a Witch is an Antichrist, opposite to Christ not only in his Works, but in his Person; for as Christ is a God incarnate: so is a Witch (as it were) a Divell incarnate. I do not say, a Witch is the Antichrist; but I am sure, the Antichrist must needs be a Witch, 2 Thes. 2. 8. 9, 10, 11.

8. Because the blasphemy against the holy Ghost, is grounded upon an imputation of Witch-craft, Matth. 12. 24, 31. And the sin it selfe appeares (by direct literall deduction) to be a malicious imputation of the works of the Devill to God; and of the works of God to the Devill: which who are so guilty of as are Witches, that make God their Divell, and the Divell their God? as is evident to be observed, in their solemn and explicite pact or League. Neither do I know any one particular sin, to which the expression of the sin against the holy Ghost in Scriptures, with the properties that Divines make thereof, may be more aptly & precisely applyed, then to this sin of Witch-craft.

II

HOW MANY KINDES OF WITCHES MAY THERE BE CONCEIVED?

A Right beliefe of Witches cannot bee without some distinct conception of their kinds, holy Scripture (to set forth their severall kinds) reckons up 8. severall names of them at once. Deut. 8. 10. 11. Some say nine; making the first paraphrasticall description (that of causing the sonne or the daughter to passe thorow the fire) to bee a certaine species of Witch-craft: which I conceive rather to be a generall Act or Rite, of consecrating or devoting themselves & theirs to the Divells service; answerable to that which wee commonly call the Witches Covenant, Compact, or Confoederation with the Divell. Because it is still set before those other particular Acts, as if it were but some kind of preparation or disposition to them, Lev. 20. 5, 6. 2 King. 21. 6. All the rest of the Words, or Names (were it not that plenary Enumerations cannot be without distinctions) are so promiscuously used, variously translated, and indifferently interpreted, that it is hard to observe any specifique difference between them. Give me leave to ghesse at them as distinctly as I may. 1. Wee thus translate the first, One that useth divination. But the Hebrew speakes somewhat more Emphatically, One divining divinations. To shew, that such his divinations were of his own divining, or devising; who presumed, or undertook to teach or tell of things contingent and fortuitous, whether future, or absent; and what hereafter might happen to such a person, such a State; And such a one I may not amisse call the Gipsie, or fortune-telling Witch. 2. An Observer of Times. The Radicall derivation of this Word or Name is thought so various, that I know not well how to determine here, what kinde of Witch. Some conceive it from an Hebrew root that signifies to answer, being interrogated in dubious matters; and so I may say it is the Oracle Witch. Some from casting a mist before the eyes, and then is it the jugling or praestigious Witch. Some from a word of the Clouds; then is it the Astrologian, Starre-gazing, Planetary, Prognosticating Witch. Some from a word that notes a Time, and that destinate or determinate to such a purpose, as lucky, or unlucky; then is it the superstitious season-searching, or (if you will) the Time-serving Witch. 3. An Enchanter, or a chaunting Witch, using to that purpose certaine Odes, Songs, Verses, Tones, Numbers, and may signifie either the Canting or Calculating Witch. But there is a word of fuller and nearer sound to the originall, that signifies the Serpent: so may it bee the Serpentine, the venesick or Poysonous Witch. 4. Or a Witch. The Originall Word is used so promiscuously, for all manner of Witches, that makes our Translators to render it in the common English word onely. Yet doth it more narrowly import, such a kind of Witch that works partly after a poysonous, partly in a praestigious way. 5. A Charmer, and that is an Exorcist or conjuring Witch. But the Hebrew expresses it thus, one joyning Society, viz. either with the Devill, or with other Witches: and so it is the assembling or the associating Witch. 6. A Consulter with Familiar Spirits. The Hebrew intimates, one that carried the Spirit in a Bottle, a Bag, a Pitcher, and so kept it as a familiar; or rather whose

Belly heaved, and swelled, and sounded like a Bottle, whence the Devill spake or replyed: and thus is it the Gastromanticke, the Ventriloquist, or if you will, the Bottle-bellyed Witch. 7. A Wizzard, or Sciolist, that is the Magicall, Speculative, Scientiall, or Arted Witch. 8. A Negromancer; that is one that sought to the Dead, and consulted them, to know what should become of the Living. Or, that haunted Graves and Sepulchers, as well praedigiously to raise the dead, as to be praestigiously resolved by them. You may call such an one, the Mortal or the deadly Witch.

To all these Names, more then ten times might be added from other Languages, expressing the severall sorts of Witches and Witcherafts; either from their Nature, Art, power, practice, matter, form, end, author, meanes, instrument, or effect. But (because I labour all I may to bring the whole business to a Previate) I shall onely treat of such kindes or sorts of them, wherein they are more universally both comprized and distinguished.

1. According to the vulgar conceit, distinction is usually made betwixt the White and the Blacke Witch: the Good, and the Bad Witch. The Bad Witch, they are wont to call him or her, that works Malefice or Mischiefe to the Bodies of Men or Beasts: The good Witch they count him or her, that helps to reveale, prevent, or remove the same. But such consider not, that devils (with as certaine a Science and as safe a Conscience) may be distinguished into Good, and Bad, as Witches. Rather, that the accounted Good Witch, is indeed the worse and more wicked of the two. For as Satan, being a Fiend of darknes, is then worst when hee transformes himselfe into an Angel of Light: so likewise are his Ministers. Now both these working by the Devill, whereas the worst hurt that the one does, proves but to bewitch the Body, or outward man: the best helpe that the other can doe, tends and turns to bewitch the inner man or

Soule. In as much as it begets in the party to be thus holpen; either a Petition, or at least an inquisition: either a perswasion, or at least an expectation; which is a faith or assent of the same nature that the Witch now workes by. Notwithstanding all this it is objected, that the Good Witch does good, & opposes the Bad Witch, and the Devill, and therefore certainly can be none of his, nor have any dealings with him. For if Satan cast out Satan, he is divided against himselfe, how shall then his Kingdome stand? Matth. 12. 26. Are not these now the Patrons of Witches themselves that can make Scripture plead for them? To whose mis-applying it is thus replyed: That if Satan should cast out Satan spiritually, or out of the soule, here were a division indeed, and now his Kingdome could in no wise stand: But for Satan to cast out Satan corporally, or out of the Body onely; this may be done by a combination, and so his Kingdome may grow the more. For thus he agrees, and willingly yeelds to his owne Children and Instruments to be (even by them) ejected out of the Body: that so by the faith (both of the doer and receiver) he may the more easily be admitted into the Soule.

2. Witches may universally be thus distinguished into either the Arted or the Pacted Witch. The Arted Witch, or one onely speculative upon the abstruse Mirables of Nature: who by searching into her occult Qualities, her hidden powers, and secret vertues, her Sympathies and Antipathies; and by applying fitly Actives unto Passives; now urges nature so Artificially, that he makes her conclude & assent to work wonders: (And happily thus far may proceed both with true Sciēce, & good conscience.) But what through vanity of Science, error of Conscience, lability of innocence; what through curiosity, Credulity, vain Glory, &c. is at length taken in the snare of praestigious and Diabolicall delusion. And now applies the Creature to those ends and uses; to which, either by its owne propensity, or by Gods Institution, it was never inclined. The

pacted Witch is one only Operative, about some prodigious or Praestigious things, and that only by vertue of a superstitious Compact or Contract made with the Divell, without, or against all Rules and orders of Nature, Art, or Grace.

3. A generall distinction (as touching kinds) may be of the Active, and the Passive Witch. The Active Witch I conceive to Act together with the Divell; but the Passive Witch to be Acted rather by him. One by way of Confoederation; the other by reason of some obsession, One as it were tempting the Divell; the other rather tempted by him. One as it were the Author, and the Divel the Instrument; the other but the bare Instrument, and the Divell the sole Author. One maliciously rejoycing and glorying in prodigious prankes and Exploits; the other somewhat irking and ashamed. One not infesting onely, but infecting also, by seeking to make others Witches; the other willing or wishing rather to bee unmade it selfe. Of the one kinde I reckon the Witch of Endor; 1 Sam. 28. of the other, the Damsell in the Acts, Acts 16. Yet ought even the Passive Witches to bee distinguished into the meerly, and the mixtly Passive. The meerly Passive be simply daemoniacks, but not Energumenists. That is mainly suffering, rather then Acting by the Divell: more excruciated and afflicted, then occupied or exercised by him. The mixtly Passive be not the Obsessed only, but the Operative likewise. Of more Active at first in giving up their Wills to Satans slavery, now become more Passive and led Captive by him at his will. First offering themselves freely and voluntarily; after forced, and as it were necessitated to doe his drudgery. The Divell now infesting them, if they grow slacke to infest others.

III

WHETHER THERE BE NOT SUNDRY DEGREES OF WITCHES AND WITCHCRAFTS TO BE CONSIDERED?

Originall sin indeed (being one & alike in all) admits of no variety of degrees in any. But witchcraft is an actuall, & therefore none are borne, all are made Witches. Talk they what they can of an Incubus, the Divell and the Witch produce not to witch-craft by Generation but seducement. Moreover, when by witchcraft one growes so high as the sin against the holy Ghost, ther's now no further measure (save in numericall Acts) for one Witch to exceed another. Otherwise there's no sinne (taken indefinitely) but may admit of severall Measures, and so (to every mans consideration) highten or lessen the guilt or poenalty to that subject in which it inheres.

It is worthy to be conscionably waighed; that in witchcraft there is an Inchoation, as well as a Consũmation. 1. The Inchoation or disposition to witch-craft is in superstition. The Fathers, and Schoolmen therefore are not much amisse in defining witch-craft by superstition: Making this to be the Genus, and gathering the other in all the species under it, so that no kind of Witchcraft may be named, which is not found upon superstition, and works not by it. Because in this main Act, superstition and Witch-craft both agree; to apply the Creature as means unto those ends and uses; unto which it is neither apt by its own nature, nor thereunto ordained by divine Institution. Only these two differ in degrees; for superstition is witchcraft begun, and witch-craft is superstition finished. Wherefore now, since Superstitions are the seedes of witch-crafts; and we all have in us the seeds of superstitions; how ought we then to take heede of nourishing superstitions; and those especially that bend & dispose to witch-craft? which are indeed too much to be observed in the Observations, Traditions, Opinions, Affections, Professions, Proverbs, Practises, Occupations, and Conversations of the Vulgar. Lord! how many are the sorcerous superstitions of the Many? As they are too too notorious; in observing of seasons for lucky or unlucky; in foretelling of Fortunes and destinies; in marking of Contingences and Casualties; in casting of Lots; in regarding of dreams; in making of meales, in using of sports, in securing of feares, in promoting of hopes, in curing of diseases, in making of Marriages, in taking of Journeys; and the like: All which (in truth) are grand superstitions, or petty kinds of witchcrafts. Yet are not to bee neglected neither: for without Gods good Grace, and great mercie, they easily grow to a higher measure or degree of that kind of malignity. 2. The Consummation and Completion of witch-craft, is in the Witches absolute Pact, and reall Fact, whereby it is covenanted & consented to work, not by God, not by nature; not by Art, not by reason; but by diabolicall delusions alone.

Likewise of reall and absolute Witches, there are several degrees to bee considered according to severall kindes of them. As the good Witch is to bee judged and esteemed worse then the bad; the Idolatrously pacted, worse then the Cunningly Arted, the pernitiously operative, worse then the fondly speculative:

the mischievously Active, worse then the abused Passive. For if among very Divels one may be found worse then another, Lu. 11. 26. how much more among Witches? nay even among Witches of the same kind, there are also considerable degrees or aggravations to guide a Conscience, either as touching private Estimation, or publike Censure, viz. 1. From the Time, as the inveterate Witch is to bee thought worse then the Novice. 2. Place, As a Witch at Court, is worse then a Witch in the Countrey, and a Witch in the Church worse then a Witch in her own Cell. 3. Sexe, As the Male witch is worse then the Female. For though she may be more envious and malicious; yet he has abused the Abler and Nobler Sexe. 4. Degree or Quality, as Jezabel was worse then the Witch of Endor. 5. Profession, As the Christian Witch is worse then the Pagan. 6. Office, As the Clericall is worse then the Layicke Witch. 7. Object, As to practise witch-craft on Men is worse then if on Beasts only. 8. Malicious intent, As to have made one Witch, is worse then to have bewitched many.

IV

WHAT IT IS THAT MAKES A WITCH TO BE A WITCH, AND ONE THAT MAY JUSTLY BE SO CALLED AND ACCOUNTED?

It is safe to believe that there are Witches; and that those also are of severall kindes and degrees. But very unsafe to pronounce peremptorily upon such and such for Witches; and that upon false grounds, as vulgar report, bare suspition, suspected Ancestors, decrepit age, froward affection, an ill tongue, or any casual accident or Event. Right effects are only censured with a safe Conscience, by those that are able to discerne them in their proper Causes; Now therfore 4. Causes are to be observed, al concurring to the making up of an absolute Witch, viz. God utterly deserting, the Devill delusively invading, speciall sins hereunto disposing, and the Compact throughly Compleating.

1. God the deficient Cause. His desertion was enough to make an Angell become a Devill: how much more then for a man to become a Witch? Yet all this is no adding to the Creatures malice, but onely to give it up to its owne power, that it may be knowne how evill it is, if his goodnesse bee once substracted. Nay, God is here not only a permissive, but a directive cause. For what forbids that God should not as justly

and wisely concur in this Act, as in all other evills of sinne? Yea great Reasons are to bee given both for his permission and direction herein. As, 1. for the manifestation of his owne Glory. As hee did the first Witches we read of, Exod. 7. 12. and 8. 18, 19. 2. For the tryall of the faith & patience of his Saints and Servants, Deu. 13. 1, 2, 3. 3. For the hardning of the wicked in their wilfull delusions, Exod. 7. 22. 2. Thes. 2. 9. 11. 4. For to make the Witches themselves examples of his justice both here and hereafter, Exo. 9. 12. Isa. 19. 3, 4. & 44. 25. Act. 13. 11. Revel. 21. 8. 5. For the more confusion of the Devill himselfe both in his frustration and ejection. Isa. 44. 25. Mic. 3. 6, 7. Matth. 12. 28, 29. 1 Joh. 3. 8. Acts 16. 18.

2. The principall Efficient of a Witch is the Devill, who indeed is the father of all such; and they his chiefely begotten Children. I meane it not by way of Incubus; which I cannot believe to be other then the height of all phantasticall Delusions, though the Patrons of it never so earnestly instance in those hairy ones, or shaggy ones, (for so the word sounds being either way pronounced) Lev. 17. 7. Isa. 13. 21. By which are to bee understood not devills Brats, but Devills themselves that appeared to Witches in such shapes when they worshipped them: Or in the Fawnes, Satyrs, Sylvaries or Syrens, that the Poets sing of: Or in the Legendary Stories of our Merlin or their Magdalen: Or in the Plebeian-traditions of Fairies, Elfes, and Changelings: Or in the old or latter Stories of such like Indian races. All these are not enough to move my beliefe; and so much the lesse, because they have impudently blasphemed Divum Lutherum, to be one of this brood. But when, I say, the Devill is the Father of Witches, I meane it after no other manner then as hee is of all the wicked, John 8. 44. by the seduction of sinne, not any production of nature. Yet I grant them his Children by a more speciall and mutuall adoption, and of all others most bearing his Image and similitude. And thus he goes about his

worke in their forming & framing. All Witchcrafts for their Originall, Invention, Operation, and use, being primarlly in the Devill (as the Issues of his depraved knowledge) onely he perceives that hee wants fit instruments for their execution. And therefore finding a faithlesse heart, a froward nature, a feeble Sex, an impotent age, an illiterate Education, a melancholy constitution, and a discontented condition: hee now workes further (and for his speciall purpose) to blinde the understanding more and more, to deprave the will, to inordinate the affections, to perturb the passions, to possesse the interiour, and delude the exteriour senses: and so infusing execrable suggestions, of murmuring against God, and desire of Revenge against Man; he thus though not absolutely inforces them, yet efficaciously inclines them to become Witches. And it is further to be observed, that the fittest subject or matter for him here to worke upon, are women commonly: And therefore (in Hebrew) a Witch is for the most part rendred in the Foeminine gender; and there are many proverbs like that of the Rabines, More women, more Witches. The reason hereof is rendred variously, from the Sexes Infirmity, Ignorance, Impotence of passions and Affections melancholy, solitarinesse, timorousnesse, credulity, inconstancy, &c. But let not the Male bee boasting, or secure of their Sexes Exemption or lesse disposition. For wee read of Pharaohs Magitians, Nebuchadnezzar's Astrologers, Manassehs Wizzards, of Balaam, Simon Magus, Elymas the Sorcerer, &c. As well as of Jezabel, the Witch of Endor, the Pythonisse, &c. And those the more notorious and malignantly operative Witches of the two.

3. The moving or provoking Causes, are divers sins, that more eminently dispose to witchcraft: such as are, 1. Idolatry; therefore are these two (Idolatry & witchcraft) conjoined so frequently, Lev. 20. 5, 6. 2 King. 21. 5, 6. and 23, 24. Gal. 5. 20. 2. Superstition; as is said before. 3. Swearing, and

blaspheming, Mal. 3. 5. 2 Thes. 4. 9. 4. Imprecation or cursing, and therefore to curse, is as much as to bewitch, Num. 22. 6. 5. Inordinate vagrant lusts, 2 Kings 9. 22. Nahum 3. 4. 6. Curiosity, this makes the Magicall Witch, Acts 19. 19. 7. Envy, hatred, malice, desire of revenge, Gal. 5. 20. 8. Depraved and indulged Melancholy; which notably disposes the matter to the introducing of such a forme, Isa. 13. 21. & 34. 13, 14. 9. Covetousness, poverty, &c. Mic. 3. 11. Nah. 3. 4. That all these are provocations to Witchcraft, wee have it abundantly in story, even from Witches owne Confessions. And this use are wee to make of it, that as we would not bee given over to Witchcraft: so should wee not give our selves over to those sinnes that so proximately dispose & incline us thereunto.

4. The formall cause of a Witch, is the Covenant, Compact, Contract, Confoederation, League, societie, familiarity with the Devill. Which hidden mystery of iniquitie is more generally consented to, that it is; then exactly disclosed what it is. All are ready to take the Witches Compact for granted, yet few (for ought I see) can well tell us what it is. Nay the Learnedst, are readyer to distinguish it, then to define it. So that hereupon it hath been somewhat dissented; and that moreover in regard of Satans prestigious delusion herein, ludibrious convention, prodigious profession, impious stipulation, perfidious intention, ridiculous obsignation, &c. And (in very truth) but to Discusse this said solemn Pact or League (according to probabilitie or possibilitie) as it is meerely related touching the formality or solemnity of it: were enough to settle a judicious mans faith upon the vanity of it: if not upon the nullity altogether. For thus Fryarly Authors, together with the Tradition of the vulgar, make it up like a Tale or Legend, viz. How that the Convention for such a solemne Initiation being proclamed (by some Herald Imp) to some others of the Confederation; on the Lords day or some great Holy day, or chief Festivall, they meete in some

Church neer the Font, or high Altar, & that either very Early, before the Consecrated bel hath tolld, or the least sprinkling of holy water; or else very late after all services are past and over. Where the party in some Vesture for that purpose, is presented, by some Confederate or familiar, to the Prince of Devills; sitting now in a Throne of Infernall Majesty, appearing in the form of a Man (only labouring to hide his cloven foote) To whom (after often bowing, and homage done in kissing his backe parts) a petition is presented to be received unto his Association and protection; And first (if the Witch bee outwardly Christian) Baptisme must bee renounced; and the Party must be Re-baptized in the Devills name, and a new name is also imposed by him: and here must be God-fathers too, for the Devill takes them not to be so adult, as to promise and vow for themselves. But above all, he is very busie with his long nayles, in scraping and scratching those places of the forehead, where the figne of the Crosse was made, or where the Chrisme was laid. In stead of both which, he himselfe impresses or inures the marke of the Beast, the Devills Fleshbrand upon one or other part of the Body: and teaches them to make an oyle or oyntment, of live Infants stoln out of the Cradle (before they be signed with the sign of the Crosse) or dead ones stolne out of their Graves, the which they are to boyle to a Jelly; and then drinking one part, and besmearing themselves with another, they forthwith feel themselves imprest and endowed with the faculties of this mysticall Art. Further the Witch (for his or her part) vowes, (either by word of mouth, or peradventure by writing, and that in their own blood) to give both body and soule to the Devill. To deny & defie God the Father, the Sonne, and the Holy Ghost. But especially the blessed Virgin, convitiating her with one infamous nick-name or other. To abhor the Word and Sacraments, but especially to spit at the saying of Masse. To spurne at the Crosse, and tread Saints Images under feet. And as much as possibly they may to profane all Saints Reliques, holy water, consecrated salt, waxe, &c. To bee sure to fast on Sundayes, and eate Flesh on Fridays, not to confesse their sinnes however they do; especially to a Priest. To separate from the Catholike Church, and despise his Vicars primacy. To attend his nocturnall Conventicles, Sabbaths, Sacrifices. To take him for their God, worship, invoke, obey him, &c. To devote their Children to him, & to labour all they may to bring others into the same Confederacy. Then the Devill for his part promises to be always present with them, to serve them at their beck. That they shall have their wills upon any Body, that they shall have what riches, honours, pleasures they can imagine. And if any be so wary as to thinke of their future Being, he tells them they shall be Principalities ruling in the Aire; or shall but bee turned into Impes at worst. Then hee preaches to them to be mindefull of their Covenant, and not to faile to revenge themselves upon their Enemies. Then he commends to them (for these purposes) an Impe, or Familiar, in the shape of a Dogge, Cat, mouse, rat, Weafle, &c. After this they shake hands, embrace in armes, dance, feast & banquet, according as the Devill hath provided in Imitation of the Supper. Nay, oft times he marries them ere they part, either to himselfe, or their Familiar, or to one another, and that by the Book of Common prayer (as a pretender to witchfinding lately told me in the Audience of many.) After this they part, till the next great conventicle or Sabbath of theirs, wch is to meet thrice in a year, conveyed as swift as the winds from remotest places of the Earth, where the most notorious of them meet to redintegrate their Covenant, & give accoũt of their Improvement. Where they that have done the most execrable mischiefe, and can brag of it, make most merry with the Devill, and they that have been indiligent, & have done but petty services in comparison, are jeered and derided by the Devill and all the rest of the company. And such as are absent, and have no care to be assoygned, are amerced to this paenalty, so to be beaten on the palms of their feete, to be whipt with iron rods, to be pincht and suckt by their Familiars till their heart blood come, till they repent them of their sloath, and promise more attendance and diligence for the future. Thus you see what we are likely to attain to, by searching too precisely into Diabolicall solemnities; amongst some probabilities to manifold Impossibilities, & absurdities, among some truths, to manifold superstitions.

But laying aside all curiosity (as indeed not necessary) in seeking to informe or resolve our selves of the form or manner of this Diabolicall Compact: wee may with moderation content our selves, that some reality is to be conceived, amongst many praestigious Delusions. A substantiall Covenant, notwithstanding all the fallacious Ceremonies. Though nothing but Impostures in the principall Agent, yet reall Depravation in the rationall Instrument. For albeit this mysticall Leviathan will make no faithfull Covenant, Job. 41. 4. nor can because of the irreconcileable emnity, Gen. 3. 15. neither will indeed bee bound to be a Servant, to bee compelled at the Witches command: neverthelesse to inshare-such in their superstition, may hee simulate the same. And after the working of Satan, with all power and signes and lying wonders, and deceivablenesse of unrighteousnesse; God may send them strong Delusions, that they may beleive a lye. 2 Thess. 2. 9, 10, 11. Likewise the Spirit speaketh expresly, that in the latter times some shall depart from the Faith, giving heed to seducing Spirits and Doctrines of Devills. 1. Tim. 4. 1. Neither is there any doubt to bee made, but that a Covenant may be made with death, and an Agreement with Hell, Esa. 28. 15. and that fellowship may be had with Devills themselves, 1 Cor. 10. 20. wee know well that the Tempter is ready to propose both the Condition and the Reward of a Compact, Matt. 4. 9. And wee heard before that one name of Witches is to bee called Joyners or Consociators, scil. not onely among themselves, but with the Devill also. Besides the Devil is Gods Ape, and one that faines to imitte him though in contrary wayes. And therefore as God makes a Covenant of Grace with his: so doth the Devill with his a Covenant of Death. Neither indeed is the universall Confession of Witches themselves (touching such a compact) to be disregarded. For who knowes the guilt of their owne Consciences better then they themselves? and though they tell us of never so much Delusion, yet can wee conceive the corruption that is in it. Nor yet is the consent and experience of all Ages to bee rejected: that tells us of such Facts of Witchcraft, as must necessarily be concluded to follow the same. For where any extraordinary or wonderous thing is done; and that neither by the power of God, nor of the good Angels; nor by the power of Nature, nor of Art; it must needs be done by the power of the Devill. And in the Instrument that doth it either the force of a possession, or the vertue of some Part, is necessarily to bee supposed which is briefely thus to bee discerned. The Devill may worke the first way upon a man against his will to punish and torment him: But he workes not with him, at his will, or to serve him; but the second way alone.

Such a Covenant or compact is unanimously delivered by the Learned, to bee two fold; Explicite, and Implicite. 1. Explicite, or Expresse, by word or writing; wherein it is mutually stipulated; the witch to doe the Devills will; and the Devill to doe the witches will and all this more visibly, formally and ceremonially Confirmed. 2. Implicite or more secret: which is conceived, may be done divers wayes; as first, by a meer Assent that the Devill should doe it, and saith that he will doe it. 2. By a Proxey, yeilding and assenting to receive and use, Rules, signes, and meanes from other Witches, without any immediate vow or Conference as yet. 3. By using superstitious Innovations, or

Imprecations, witha perswasion or Expectation of their Issue. 4. By employing meanes to those purposes, to which God never appointed them, nor their owne nature enclined them; and yet confident of their Effect. 5. By seeking too, and consulting with Witches for their advice, helpe, &c. For there is the same faith and assent now both of the Consulter and the Practiser. 6. By assenting to use such meanes and signes as witches also use: (viz. Charms, Spells, Characters, Figures, Circles, Ligatures, words, phrases, Ceremonies, gestures, &c.) not well considering the superstitious institutions, but peradventure perswaded of some real vertue in them. For even Witches themselves make certain Confections (as Broths, oyles, unguents, powders, &c.) the vertue whereof they impute not solely to the Devil, but partly to the things themselves.

Now let Witches be Examined upon these two maine Grounds of their making: and where one is so become after an explicite manner of Covenanting; more then ten of them are guilty after the Implicite and Invisible way onely. And there is this Difference (which would be noted) between them. The Explicite Covenanter is the notorious and audacious; the Implicite but a Novice and a Bastard in comparison. The Explicite hath alwayes some visible or sensible familiarity; so hath not the implicite as yet. The Explicite is become a perpetuall witch; the Implicite may onely be but so for that present Act, or time being: onely this is to be feared; the Implicite being hardned a while, may grow to be Explicite at length.

V

WHAT ARE THE SIGNES AND MARKES OF A WITCH, WHEREBY SUCH AN ONE MAY BE RIGHTLY DISCERNED, AND SO CENSURED?

Signes of a Witch are either true or false; right or wrong: And this is a signe that Ignorant and ill men have presumed to judg and censure here, as well as others; Nay, in that the received signes or markes are more false then true; more strong then right; it is a signe that such kind of men have beene more forward to censure here then others. For as the men were, so were their Markes either more or lesse advised. Amidst which variety, let me here distinguish of some unwarrantable, some probable, and some more infallible.

1. Some Marks, or Tokens of Tryall altogether unwarrantatable; as proceeding from Ignorance, humor, superstitiõ; such are, 1 The old paganish sign, the Witches long eyes. 2 The Tradition of the witches not weeping. 3 The Witches making il favored faces & mũbling. 4 To burn the thing bewitched, &c. (I am loath to speak out, lest I might teach these in reproving them.) 5 The burning of the thatch of the Witches house, &c. 6. The heating of the horseshoe, &c. 7. The scalding water, &c. 8. The sticking of knifes acrosse, &c.

9 The putting of such and such things under the Threshhold, and in the Bedstraw, &c. 10 The seive and the sheares, &c. 11 The casting the Witch into the water with thumbes & toes tyed across, &c. 12. The tying of knots, &c. If these (or the like) be signs, to try and know a Witch by; certainly it can be no other Witch but the user of them. And if it bee objected, that the expected Effect hath followed hereupon; I answer, that may be done by the Devil, not for the Witches convictions, but to nourish the other in their superstitiō. To all these I cannot but adde one at large, wch I have lately learnt; partly frō some cōmunication I had wth one of the Witchfinders (as they call them) partly from the confession (which I heard of a suspected & a Committed witch so handled as she said, & partly as the countrey-people talk of it. Having taken the suspected Witch, shee is placed in the middle of a room upon a stool, or Table, crosse legg'd, or in some other uneasie posture, to which if she submits not, she is then bound with cords, there is she watcht & kept without meat or sleep for the space of 24. hours. For (they say) within that time they shall see her Impe come and suck; a little hole is likewise made in the door for the Impe to come in at: and lest it might come in some lesse discernible shape, they that watch are taught to be ever & anon sweeping the room, and if they see any spiders or flyes, to kill them. And if they cannot kill them, then they may be sure they are her Impes. If this be true, how should it trouble us, that an invention or practise of so much folly & superstition should arise amidst so cleare a light of the Gospell? But as to the killing of the Imp, let mee further inform them, that if the Imp be of a wafted & condensed ayr, it cannot be killd, because it never had life: But if it bee a very Cat or Dogge, &c. only possessed with the Devill, it may be kild: And I have heard a Committed Witch confesse, that she kild one time her dog, another time her Cat (both her imps) for going out & doing so much mischief against her wil.

2. Some signs probable, yet not so certaine as to serve for the Witches Conviction. Such are, 1. Strong and long suspition. 2. Suspected Ancestors.

3. Bare Confession. 4. Some Appearance of Fact. 5. The corps bleeding upon the Witches touch. 6. The testimony of the party bewitched. 7. The supposed witches unusual bodily marks. 8 The witches usual cursing & banning. 9. The witches lewd & naughty kind of life.

3. Some more infallible and certaine signes. As. 1. Declining Iudieature, or Faltering, faulty, unconstant and contrary Answers; upon judiciall and deliberate examination. 2. When by a true examination (of Faith and Mannrs) there are found all or most of the causes fore-spoken of. viz. God Deserting, the Devill invading, particular sins disposing; and the Compact compleating. 3. The Witches free Confession, together with full Evidence of the Fact. For Confession without Fact, may be a meer delusiō; & Fact without Confession, may be but a meer accidēt. 4. The semblable Gestures and demeanures of Witches, with Comparable expressions of passions and affections, which in all Witches (of all Times and Places) have been observed and found to be very much alike. 5. The Testimony of the party bewitched, (whether pining or Dying) together with the joynt Oaths of sufficient persons that have seene certain prodigious prankes or feates, wrought by the party accused. 6. Haunting the houses or companyes of notorious Witches, and especially frequenting their nightly meeting. 7. Whom other notorious Witches have impeached to be as ill as themselves. 8. If noted for long dis-frequenting & neglecting the Church, or Congregation; the word preached, and Sacrament administred. 9. If it can be proved that such an one hath allured or inticed others to witchcraft. 10. A maligning & oppugning the Word, Work, and Worship of God: and by any extraordinary signe, seeking to pervert and seduce any from it. Deut. 13. 1. 2. Mat.

24. 24. Acts 13. 8. 10. 2 Tim. 3. 8. Do but marke well the places, and for this very propertie (of thus opposing and perverting) they are all there concluded to be arrant and absolute Witches.

Now to guide the Conscience in discerning and censuring; where the signes & notes (one with another) of the last sort are found; there (as touching the Witch) it may safely be pronounced and proclaimed. Where those of the second only are; there may bee some suspition or estimation, and that irreprehensible. But wher no note of Tryal is to be found, save only those of the first sort, there it is egregious Calumny, and infamy irreparable. We therefore approve of the last, admit of the second, but altogether condemn the first. Yet (as touching the second) there is need of some Caution, because it is much upon suspition. (And all suspition whatsoever, cannot be but unsafe to Conscience, if it want the due Caveats) What Conscience then can here bee in common people that are carryed away not onely with suspition but superstition? Every poore and peevish olde Creature (such is their Ignorance and Uncharitablenesse) cannot but fall under their suspition, nay their infamous exprobation; every Accident, (more then ordinary) every disease whereof they neither understand the Cause, nor are acquainted with the Symptomes) must bee suspected for witch-craft. His Cow or his Hog, cannot be strangely taken, but straight it must bee reckoned and rumored for bewitcht. And now their ill will to the next neighbouring silly Creature, must peremptorily taxe her ill will (in the worst sense) for the only cause of all. A bare Casualty, or accidental effect (especially if any thing touches them in their owne particular) shall now bee to them a more sure and certaine Token of the Witch, then all the marks that Learning and Experience speakes of besides. And there's no staving them off their owne conceited way of Tryall, though it bee never so unwarrantable, never so unlawfull. And but to advise them to prudence and Conscience in such a case; is to be reputed and reported, a Patron, a Pleader, a Favourer and a Flesher of Witches. But men that are either conscientious or judicious, will not easily harbour a suspition (either in this or any other thing) unless it bee from some very shrewd signes, probable reason, frequent Experience: nor will they lightly admit of any report (bee it never so old, so common) unlesse it bee also from the well reported.

VI

WHETHER WITCH-SEEKING, OR WITCH-FINDING BE AN ART, VOCATION, PROFESSION, OCCUPATION, OFFICE, OR TRADE OF LIFE, ALLOWABLE IN A CHRISTIAN CHURCH OR STATE?

This Case is new; because such a Profession or occupation has not beene heard of heretofore. And therfore since I am to venture where the path is not troden, I shall willingly yield to any that can shew mee a directer way to truth in this particular; then that which I now propose. Distinguishing here betwixt the Authority, the Art, and the office of Witch-finding, and thereupon thus determining.

1. That the Authority (of Governors in Church and State) is (to such a purpose as Witch-searching or Witch-finding) not onely Lawfull, but laudable: not onely warrantable, but commendable withall. In Deut. 18. 10. There shall not be found among you scil. Gods People, &c. This imports an Authority from God to seek out such; Else how should it be knowne, whether such were to bee found amongst them yea or no; In 1 Sam. 28. 7. Sauls Authority injoyning his Servants (Seeke me a woman that hath a Familiar Spirit) was not unwarrantable, but his purpose onely. But every way commendable was Josiahs

spying out of such, 2. King. 23. 24. as intirely both proceeding from obedience, and tending to Reformation.

2. That the Art of Witchfinding is very Difficult. 1. Because Satan is subtile, and has even here a 1000 deluding Arts, and wayes. 2. Most men are ignorant of his Stratagems, enterprizes, devices, 3. Witchcraft it selfe is a darke mystery of iniquitie. 4. It is so particular a Depravation, that it can hardly be ghest at or imagined by any semblance of those common feeds of corruptions that are in Men. 5. Even Witches themselves are ignorant of this their owne Art. 6. The true markes of a Witch (or mentall Characters) are not easie to be discerned.

3. That the office of Witchfinding is exceeding doubtful, Because he that offers to take upon him such an office, cannot (I am afraid to give satisfaction to these doubts, and the like. 1. Though peradventure hee may have procured some Authoritie from men: yet whether he be hereunto called and inabled by God; 2. Whether he is able to execute it with a good conscience voyd of offence both towards God, and towards men; 3. Whether he have any certaine and infallible Rules of Discerning to proceed by; 4. Whether (in this undertaking) he aim not more at a privat Advantage, then at the publick Good? 5. Whether he often times uses not unlawfull and indirect meanes of Discoverie; or incourages not the Common People to use the same? 6 Whether hee may not give occasion to Defame Ten that are Innocent; before he descover one that is guilty? 7. Whether his Carriages in this business, may not be a great occasion to augment the vulgar Peoples superstitions (and very dangerously superstitious) opinions, suspitions, traditions, perswasions, affections, admirations, and Relations? (I propose this to be well considered, because the Country People talke already, and that more frequently, more affectedly, of the infallible and wonderfull power of the Witchfinders; then they doe of God, or Christ, or the Gospell preached). 8. Whether

peremptorily to pronounce before-hand what multitudes of Witches are to be found in every Country of England, be not (besides a wicked Calumny,) an irreparable Infamie to the Church of England, in causing the adversaries of the Reformed Religion to blaspheme?

Besides all this; I require full satisfaction in these Doubts also: For I am not satisfied: that such an office ought to be taken upon them by any privat persons, as a Calling, Profession, occupation or Trade of Life. Because, if any Lawfulnesse be in such a kind of Calling; it must either be as ordinary, or as extraordinary.

1. I conceive, not as an Ordinary calling, 1. Because ordinary Callings have ordinary Principles, Grounds, Precepts, Rules, Documents, Prescriptions, Directions, Examples, Presidents, Exercises, Practises, &c. 2. Ordinary Callings have Ordinary Derivations, Propagatious, Continuation, &c. 3. Wee worthily confute the Papists, for setting up the office or Calling of an Exorcist, as Ordinary and constant in the Church. Of whose Office are two maine Acts; one to discerne, discover, and descry the Devill and the Witch: the other to adjure, charme, expell, remove &c. The former of which Acts is here confest; and if any Formes of adjuration bee used in the Examination or Discovery, the other is not to be denied. And how wary must hee bee here in Examining, that would take heed of Adjuring? 4. As touching the second Act of such an Office, the Scripture plainly denyes an ordinary or settled Calling, saying They are Vagabonds, that they tooke it upon them, and for this cause it is demanded, Who are ye? that is, where's your calling or power thus to do? Acts 19. 13, 14, 15. And therefore may the first Act very well be doubted of.

2. Not as Extraordinary. For 1. The Extraordinarily Called, are raised and separated, immediately, eminently, miraculously: 2. And that upon extraordinary occasions; as when the Church

of God is thereby extreamely infested, infected, obscured, indangered. 3. Such are evermore by God prepared, gifted, strengthened, maintained, perfected.

All that can bee objected to me is; How then would you have Witches found out? I answer, by the power of the Magistracy and Ministery; appointing and employing (upon evident and urgent necessity, as when not only common Reports, but prodigious Facts cry out) fit persons to such a purpose. I say fit; both for number and Quality. 1. For number, Competent. Not one or two obscure persons, A man with a woman, &c. But even a sufficient number, the better to Examine, Reason, Debate, Discern, Determine; in case of particular Respects, Ends, fancies, opinions, humours, Passions, Affections, &c. 2. For Quality, meet Persons for that purpose, which ought not to be, 1. Ignorant, 2. Profane. 3. Covetousnesse. But ought to be, 1. Conscientious, 2. Discreet. 3. Learned. And Learned, very learned. 1. In naturall Philosophy, that they may discern betwixt things meerly praestigious, and the Mirables of Nature, in her occult Qualities, Sympathies, Antipathies, and apt conjunction of Actives to Passives. Through Ignorance whereof, a Country Fellow is ready to cry a Witch, or a thing done in the Devills name, if hee see one make iron to walke after him, though by vertue of a Loadstone. Or to create fire in a wide field, though it be by force of a burning glasse, so he would in ignorant manner think all bewitcht, that his ship should stand immoveable, and nothing to hinder it, but a slender Remora. So would an Indian, when he sees a man from a great Gunnes mouth, fall down dead, more then a mile off. 2. In physicke; to judge of Facts and Effects (in Men or Beasts) whether naturall, preternaturall, &c. For how apt are ordinary people to apprehend the strange handlings in Extasies, Frenzies, Lunaries, Lethargies, convulsions, falling sicknesses, &c. to bee no other then very Witchcrafts. 3. In Divinity, to examine the conscience by the Rules of the word, & dictates of right reason; & to discern & declare how utterly opposite the diabolicall Covenant is, to the Covenant of Grace. 4. In Law, to declare who are here lyable, and how far; & to what kinds or degrees of guilt or penalty.

Now that such as these (upon due occasion) are the only requisite and approvable for such a purpose: and that even they themselves shall find this undertaking a matter of no smal difficulty; will plainly appear if the principal groūds of a Witches discovery be wel considered; which are either from suspition, confession, compact, practise, markes, or imps. As touching I suspition, whether causeless, or reasonable. Or the extent of suspition whether generall or particular. Or the person suspecting, whether idle, or of honest repute. Or the person suspected; whether his or her eminent vertues or graces, will admit of such a thing, yea or no?

2. Confession; How warily would it be considered; if the party confessing bee of right mind: and not diabolically deluded to confesse not improbabilities only, but impossibilities: if it be not forced, but a free confession. If Melancholy Humors, work not too fond and false self-perswasions. If they may not be some seeds of superstitiō disposing to witchcraft only; whereof the Conscience convicted and distracted, errs confusedly in apprehending and acknowledging all the Completion thereof.

3. Compact; whether the League or Covenant made with the Devill be Explicite and solemn; or Implicite and secret. If Implicite only; whether an Implicite pact (being but a bare asset of the mind or wil) serve utterly to renounce God & Christ, &c. And to joyn in full society and familiarity with the Devill? And whether all sins of malice, are not guilty in some degree of the like renuntiation and Confederacy.

4. Practise; whether no Magicall, sorcerous Charming, Conjuring, praestigious Acts, can be done without a diabolicall

Confoederacie? whether every Effect of malefice and mischiefe that is immediately consequentiall to a Cursed Tongue, be to be censured as a work of direct witchcraft? whether of wondrous and dismall Events, some be not to be referred to the Mirables of nature; some to contingencie & casualty; some to divine judgment, some to Diabolicall obsession, as well as some to Effascination? whether the Devill may not work the Facts & Effects of witchcraft; by such as only stand as yet, but in the Temptation, or some disposition to be Witches? whether the devil (as author) may not worke some particular effects of mischief, against the Wil & Intention of the Instrument?

5. Markes. Whether the expresse Character of a Witch be Corporall or Mentall; Whether all Witches have Corporall Markes, or diabolicall Flesh-brands? Whether all Witches Flesh Markes be alike in every part, and so to be known by Comparison? Whether the Devill sets his express and visible seale, upon the Implicite and invisible Compact? How may it be discerned betwixt this Devills body-mark, and any other Corporall Infirmitie? I have hard it Traditionally Fabled of the strange figure, color, noysomenesse, bloodlesness, searedness, deadnesse, &c. yet to mee it is nothing Argumentative. But I will help them to one which (I take it) is demonstrative. viz. If the Learned Physician can solidly conceive and aver that such a thing can have no naturall cause from the Body, nor can be of any Issue or use to the Body; then it argues and Demonstrates something indeed. For the Devills Brandes perish utterly, and are lost to any naturall use of the Body; as being imprest and muted to serve for no other purpose, but as Seals to the Devills Sacrament alone. Lastly, what man (of never so much observation or Experience) can with a safe conscience take his oath directly, that such Markes are imprest by the Devill, and serve onely for his use?

6. Imps, whether all Witches have their Imps or deale with

Familiars? whether a visible Impe be given upon an Invisible Compact? whether the Impe workes at the Witches, or at the Devills Command or Instigation? How can a Familiar or Impe be discerned, if it never did any thing, but what (by nature, or Art) a Creature of that same kind, may stand in a Capacity to do? who can flatly atest wth a good Conscience; that this or that Dog, Cat, Rat, Mouse, &c. is the Witches Imp or Familiar?

These things being considered (with many moe almost irresoluble scruples, that might pertaine to this scrutiny) I see not but that I may conclude? Though the Authority be commendable, yet the Case is doubtfull, the undertaking difficult, the profession dangerous, but the usurpation damnable.

VII

WHETHER ALL SUCH FEATES, TRICKES, PRANKS, AND EXPLOITS, AS WITCHES ARE SAID TO PLAY; BE CREDIBLE TO PRUDENT CHRISTIANS?

The Feates or prankes of Witches, are nothing else, but an applying of unnaturall and unapt meanes, and unappointed by God, to bring some strange, odde or infrequent, some prodigious, stupendous or wondrous things to passe; and present them to the outward senses. The more light and Triviall of them are done by the Witchmaking; having an Imp (as an Ape) ready to play such tricks at a becke, or a nodde. But the more prodigious or stupendous are effected meerly by the Devill; the witch all the while either in a Rapt, ecstasie, a charmed sleepe, or a melancholy Dreame: and the Witches imagination, phantasie, common sense, only deluded with what is now done, or pretended.

All which Feats might be referred to the Witches Compacts, Conventicles, or common practises. And though Learned men (that write volumes of this subject) be much upon them, yet I (that intend but an Abstract) list not to belong upon the Legend of Witches. And therefore forbeare to order them: and shall onely give a Tast of them confusedly, and one amongst another.

They tel us (and the vulgar second them with numberles Traditions) of their reading in the moon, al things that shall come to passe for a Thousand Generations. Of their reading by star-light, what another has writtē in his Closet a Thousand miles off. Of causing the voyces of two in Conference to be mutually heard although as distant one from another as the East is from the West. Of their being metamorphosed, or turned into Beasts, Bears, Dogs, Wolves, Goats, Catts, Hares, &c. of their cutting one anothers heads off, and setting them on again; suffering their Limbs to be pluck tasunder and knitting thē to again immediatly. Of their flying in the Aire: and walking invisible. Of their riding long and tedious Fourneys upon Broomes and Distaffes? and their sayling over seas in Eggshells. Of their carnall Copulation with the Devill; and what feat Elfes and Changelings of such a Coition; now as bigge as Gyants, and anon as little as Pigmeyes. Of their Eating up whole Fields of Corn or hay, & drinking up whole rivers in seives. Of presenting a Curious Banquet upon the Table; and inviting thereto their Guests out of Fairy Land. Of making a garden of delicat flowers to spring up in your Parlour in the dead of winter. Of raising Stormes and showres out of Tubs, turning Streams backward; haling Ships laden against Wind and water, with Haires or twined Threads. Of making a Cock or a Flye to draw the hugest Beame. Of giving Potions to make people love or hate as they please. Making the strength of youth impotent, and dead Bodies viripotent. Of making bodies impenetrable or shot-free; annoynting the Weapon, and curing the wound, without the least virtuall Contiguity: And turning all Metalls into Gold, Drinking off a glasse of Clarret, and make it to spout out of the forehead presently. Shewing you such and such Faces in Glasses &c. Causing to daunce naked &c. What should I tell of their Feates wrought by Figures, Characters, Spells, Ligatures, Circles, Numbers, Barbarismes, Images of wax or clay, Crystalls, looking-glasses, Basons of waters, herbs, powders, urguments, sawes, knives, pins, needles, Candles, rings, garters, gloves, &c. I feare I have even cloyd, while I talked but of giving a Tast.

A wise Christian and Conscientious wil leave the faith of all or most of these matters, with the Authors. No prodigious Acts (though avouched and attested by hundreds and Thousands) must impose upon his Beleife: If they utterly thwart his eternall and infallible Rules of Truth, which are,

1. To beleve, that all the Devills stupendous Actions in this kind, are praestigious Delusions. That is, either meerly Delusive, where all else is impossible, but the Delusion it selfe: or mixtly delusive, where peradventure amongst some reality of meanes, matter, event, there is nothing but praestigiousnesse of Forme, End, Effect.

2. To believe nothing of all these, that (in the least) do usurp or trench upon the divine Attributes; omniscience, omnipotence, &c. For though Devills be intelligential creatures, and of admirable Ingeny and sagacity in comparison to reasonable Souls; yet while (their Intellect was unobscured by their Fall) all their perspicacity never reached to a shadow of Omniscience: much lesse can all their long Experience, Observation, or Revelation, now attain to it. And therfore if they foresee of thēselves, or foretel some kind of Futures; it is but as they are contain'd in their natural causes, or dispositions: And if they ghess at some secret intentions or affectiōs of the heart, it is no more then from certaine outward motions. So that wee may well conclude, they are ignorant, and erre in very many things; whereof the Ambiguity of their propositions and predictions, are a sufficient Confession.

Likewise, though Devils be called Principalities and powers, & that no power on earth may be compared to them; yet was all their power (ere debilitated by their fall) of no force to that power that belongeth unto God; Wonders they may worke, but those lying ones, Deut. 3. 2. Mat. 24. 24. 2 Thes. 2. 9. And yet not those, but as permitted by God, not Impedited by Angels, and having the matter hereunto somwhat praedisposed. And even then it is (for the most part) praestigious too. Illuding humane senses, abusing their Fancies, and (which is worse) deceiving their hearts. Their utmost is but to produce phantasmaticall or false species of things; and if any thing bee now verily done, it is but by applying Actives to Passives: which if wee were as cunning in as they; we might also doe without them, and need never be beholding to them. But as for Miracles (of a true name and thing) they are as strange and as admirable to them, as they are to us. And indeede neither for them, nor us, nor for Angells to do, but for God alone, Psal. 72. 18. He only can work miracles, to whom nothing is a Miracle. And it were easie (were it not too long) to distinguish betwixt divine Miracles, and Diabolical Prodigies; both from the dignity and vertue of the doere; the Quality, Excellency of the thing done, with the admirable and advantagious manner and end of doing.

3. To believe nothing of these, that (being granted) must of necessity work the universall disorder and confusion of nature. For though the Devill may haply bee able to perturbe some particular course of Nature: yet (Devils themselves, being part of the Universe) have no power to worke to the Confusion and destruction of the whole.

4. To beleeve nothing of them, that utterly impugn the dictates of right Reason. For that would directly imply contradictions; and then impossibilities are necessarily to be concluded.

5. Not to beleeve any thing of these, contrary to the infallible Rules of Gods word. For what Faith can bee of those things, that crosse the grounds of Faith? Against which eternall Rules of truth (whether of precept, promise, or practise) Devills and

men, in all their Operations or Testimonies must needes bee found Lyars.

6. Nothing must be believed of all these, as tending to truth or to God. For the Devill is false, and can speak no trueth, but to deceive; and the Devil is naught, and will do nothing like to Good, but to hurt and endamage so much the more.

VIII

WHETHER THE POWER OF A WITCH BE SUCH AS IS ORDINARILY SUPPOSED?

If we would be ledde by the terrible Traditions, Opinions, and apprehensions of the vulgar; they are mostly ready to imagine, the power of a Witch, to be more like the power of a Devill, then of a Witch: and so, the power of a Devill to be more like the power of a God, then of a Devil. And are eftsoones affrayd of the power of the Devill, more then of GOD: And of the WITCH more then of the DEVILL: yea and (out of that feare) are readyer to serve and please the Devill and the Witch, then God himselfe. But to be better informed, let us here inquire,

1. Whence have Witches all their power? And I say, firs, Not of God. For this is it chiefely that makes the Act to be forcerous and prodigious, that the wounder is wrought, but not by the power of God. Yet I dare not say, this power of theirs (what ever it is) is not from God. For the evil Spirit was from the Lord, that troubled & terrified Saul. 2 Sam. 16. 14. Neither did Satan touch, Job, (body or goods) but as God gave him, once and againe into his hands. Job. 1. and 2. Nor had all the Devills power to enter into or infest the swine, but as Christ was pleased to permitt. Mar. 5. 12. whence I conclude that God hath even.

here also a working power: viz. of permission, Limitation, Direction, yea & of Cooperation; and yet all this without the least approbation of the power abused by the Devill or the Witch. 2. Not from good Angells. For good Angells and Witches never worke one with another: Because Witches work by vertue of a Compact, to adore the Power that they work by: and that the Good Angells can in no wise indure. Revel. 19. 10. Neither (though they may be Instruments of Gods just judgements) can they be assistant to the malice and iniquity of the Creature. Neither yet will the Excellency and Ingenuity of good Angels, suffer them to condescend (upon any tearms between them) or dissemble a being bound at a vile wretches beck. How much deceived then (through Satans transformation of himself) are those Witches that have imagined their Familiars to be no other then good Angels? 3. Not from Nature. For they take her un-aptest means; and apply them to the wrongest ends. 4. Not from Art, or Science. Because they are indeed ignorant of all such grounds and principles; rules & reasons. 5. Al their power therefore must needes bee from the devil only; who conveys unto them, what power is permitted him in that particular; by vertue of a cursed Contract, or confederation. In the execution wherof, he himselfe nevertheless is the sole agent; and they but the wretched InInstruments. For (as the Hebrew hath it of the Witch of Endor, 1 Sam. 28. 7. and is plainly rendred, Nahum 3. 4.) though they seeme Ladies and Mistresses of their Arts & acts; yet are they indeed but Satans meer slaves and Vassals. Commanding openly that power, as if they were superiour to him: and yet secretly invoking it, as inferior. And so the Devill seemes as if hee were now compelled to obey; when hee cunningly dissembles it, for his own ends. Only he is willing to have this power both to be challenged by them, and imputed to them: that so hee may transfer upon them, the guilt, and hatred, of all those Mischiefs & Malignities, both before God, and men.

2. After what manner doe they use to exercise their power of bewitching? Sometimes they practise their power with more Formality; sometimes with lesse. Now on a sodain & all at once; now by times and degrees. Some by themselves, some with their fellow Witches. Sometimes after this manner, and by these means: sometimes by the clean contrary. As witnesses (what from confession, and Tradition) their sundry bewitching places, Seasons, Vestures, Gestures, Postures, Spells, Characters, Ligatures, Signes Images, Confections, herbs, unguēts, meats, drinkes, powders, boylings, broylings, scaldings, burnings, buryings, &c. Indeed, what Act or Instrument of Man, can be named; that has not been, or may not be, sorcerously abused? Let me instance more expresly in a few particulars, 1. Some worke their bewitchings only by way of Invocation, or Imprecation. They wish it, or will it; and so it falls out. 2. Some by way of Emissary; sending out their Imps, or Familiars, to crosse the way, justle, affront, flash in the Face, barke, howle, bite, scratch, or otherwise infest. 3. Some by Inspecting, or looking on, but to glare, or squint, or peep at with an envious and evill eye, is sufficient to effascinate. (Especially Infants & women with Child.) 4. Some by a demisse hollow muttering or mumbling, Isa. 8. 19. & 29. 4. 5. Some by breathing & blowing on; the usuall way of the venefick. 6. Some by cursing & banning. 7. Some by blessing and praising. 8. Some revengefully, by occasion of ill turns. 9. Some ingratefully, and by occasion of good turnes. 10. Some by leaving something of theirs in your House. 11 Some by getting something of yours into their House. 12. Some have a more speciall way of working by severall Elements; Earth, water, ayre, or fire. But who can tell all the manner of wayes of a Witches working; that works not only darkly and closely, but variously & versatilly, as God will permit, the Devil can suggest, or the malicious Hag devise

to put in practise?

3. Upon whom do Witches execute their power? If wee can credite what is reported of the old Pagan Witches; how they threaten the Gods, the Heavens, Sphears, Planets, Elements, &c. To pull downe the Sun, Moon, and Stars, and preserve their Influences in Boxes, to mingle all, and make a new Chaos, to dry up the Seas, and remove Mountains, &c. Nay and some of our later Witches are wont to brag of a power they have over the Devill himselfe, how they can compell him, chain him, whip him, torment him. And these are they the Papists call Exorcists, which we call Conjurers. Who are said to differ from other kinde of Witches in this, that they can imperiously command the Devill, &c. Whereas others are glad to do all by Invocation or Intreaty. Indeed Christ gave his Disciples an extraordinary power against him, Mar. 3. 15. and 16 17. and for anything that hee can do against us, hath left us the ordinary means, 1 Pet. 5. 8, 9. But I would these kinde of people could as easily extricate themselves out of the Devills power: as wee (for Trueths sake) must vindicate him from theirs. And that 1. Because a Creature that is inferiour by Nature, cannot (without a divine power) compell one that is superiour to it.

2. A pretence to or usurpation of a Divine power against him, prevayles not to subject him, but inrage him rather, as Act. 19. 13, 14, 15, 16. 3. It is not likely the Devill would invent or deliver any such Art, whereby himself might verily bee coarcted or constrained: who is of such a pride as can indure to be brought into no subjection or obedience; whether to God, or Men.

But thus much is to be beleived even by knowing Christians. That witches may have a power from the Devill to perturbe all things sublunary. And therefore they, and the Devill are not amisse sayd to move winds, Storms, Tempests, showrs, Lightnings, (and some say Thunders) hayle, snow, Frosts, mists,

Foggs, smokes, Blastings, Skathfires, Earthquakes, Seawracks, Sicknesses, Diseases &c. (I spare to speak of their more notorious power over things inanimate, vegetables and all brute Creatures) But as touching Mankind (for there's all the spite of the Devill, and the Witch) that abuse not the other Creatures, but in his prejudice. Concerning such, it is commonly said, that witches have power over Infants, more then the Aged; over Women, more then over men; and over women with Child, more then over others. And for the proof wee are put to story, Tradition, and Experience. But the Question (best worth deciding in the whole Case) is this. Whether Witches have any power against faithful & godly men: as well as against the Wicked and profane. Some people are perswaded, that a Witch can have no power at all against a faithfull man. And think themselves armed sufficiently to their opinion, from a great Witches owne Confession. Numbers, 23. 23. Surely there is no enchantmēt against Jacob, nor is there any Divination against Israel. But it would be considered, that the Hebrew word signifies (Notice) rather then (not against:) yea but say, not against Jacob, not against Israel; Iacob and Israel there intimate a Congregation, not a person. Thus therefore it may truly be distinguished, & determined; That Witches and Sorcerers can have no power against the whole Church of God, the whole body of Christ, but may doubtles over this or that particular person; though never so pious, never so beleeving. Because such a subjection, followes Gods permission. And being but a temporall evill, no faith or piety hath here an absolute promise of Exemption: Satan had his obsessing power even over Job, a Godly man; as well as over Saul, a wicked man. Christ acknowledges one for a daughter of Abraham, and withall that she was troubled with a spirit of Infirmity, Luk. 13. That is, an Infirmity wrought by the meanes of an evill Spirit. How easy were it (but that I resolve against all such prolixity) to instance from the

Fathers, and other Authors, of more then Hundreds of good and Godly men (in all Ages) not onely immediatly obsessed by the Devill; but by his evill Instruments, most strangely and terribly bewitcht? Besides Examples and experience, there is reason also to establish this for a Truth, 1. Because Corporal bewitching is (as I said) but an outward suffering; against which not the best Saint hath any Ground to plead an absolute priviledg. 2. One of the maine Reasons of Gods permission of Witches were thus eluded. viz. For the Try-all of the Faith and patience of the Saints, which, how could it possible be, if they were here Exempted? 3. The Devills hatred is greatest a gainst Godly men, whom he labors most (by himselfe and his Instruments) to disturbe and Distract. Yet in this Community of sufferance, is there some difference to be observed. As the Godly are bewitched in their Body onely: the Wicked both in body and soule. The Godly for the Try-all of their Graces: the Wicked for the punishment of their Sins. The wicked Curse God to his face: the Godly blesse him so much the more. To the Godly, this is all their Hell: to the Wicked, but as their Hells beginning.

IX

HOW THE POWER AND MALICE OF WITCHES MAY BE PREVENTED AND REDREST WITH A GOOD CONSCIENCE?

The Popish Schoolemen not a little leave our Consciences perplexed, in this Question of theirs. Whether it be lawfull to remove the signes of Witchcraft; to the Intent the Effect thereof may cease? In that they who proposed it, are so divided upon it. Some of them make it an Act meritorious, so to doe: Some againe, an Act Superstitious. But their Resolution on either side satisfies not. For it cannot be an Act meritorious in any (to dispell or destroy the signs, means & works of the Devill) but in him alone that came into the world for that very intent. 1 John. 3. 8. Nor is it to be counted for an Act superstitious, to remove or dissolve any thing, that the Witch hath left or put in any place, for a Signe, Spell, Charme to bewitch by; and that such a thing removed, dissolved, the Witchcraft is disappointed and must cease. So be, it be certain that they are the signes or meanes of witchcraft, and placed there for that very End. And that there bee not a more diligent search to find out the Witches signe or spell, then to betake to prayers and like duties. And that the Effect of such ceasing bee not hoped or expected meerly from the Removall of the thing; nor as the Consequent or Condition of the diabolicall Compact. But that it is done through Confidence in God; and a contempt of all such Sorceries. For if a man were certaine that such a thing were a Witches signe or spell to bewitch by; it would argue more assent to the Devils working to suffer it, and let it alone; then to remove or destroy it. Neither is there any doubt to bee made, but that Witchcraft (with all the Appendices) may be resisted and removed by any unlawful meanes. Which cannot but be such, if there be no consulting with, cōsēting to, or expecting from the Devill: but a Reference to, confidence in, and dependance upon God alone.

Indeed people are here but too superstitious, as touching the Fortifying or relieving themselves. I passe over what superstitious Remedies are here taught in that other Religion; as the tolling of a baptized bell; signing with the signe of the Crosse, sprinkling with holy water, blessing of Oyle, Waxe, Candles, Salt, Bread, Cheese, Garments, weapons, &c. carrying about saints Reliques, with a thousand superstitious fopperies of their exorcising Trade. I only speak of such superstitious practises, as are used by men of all Religions. 1. In seeking to a witch, to be holpen against a Witch. 2. In using a certain or supposed Charme; against an uncertaine or suspected witchcraft. 3. In searching anxiously for the Witches signe or Token left behinde her in the house, under the Threshold, in the Bedstraw: and to be sure to light upon it, burning every odd ragge or bone, or feather that is to be found. 4. In swearing, rayling, threatning, cursing, and banning the Witch: as if this were a right way, to bewitch the Witch from Bewitching. 5. In Banging and basting, scratching & clawing, to draw blood of the witch: an Act not onely superstitious, but so injurious; that it's rather a provocation to the malice of the witch, then any Fortification against it. 6. In daring and defying the Witch out of a Carnall security, and presumptuous temerity: Believe well (saythey) have a good heart and feare not, and the Witch can have no power over, &c. A good Beliefe will now arme well indeed: But alass! that's quite another thing, to this confident Audacity. One is in God, the other in themselves. One is the Confidence of a pure heart, the other is the security of the profane: One keepes within its own Calling, the other wanders out of it: And so not only tempts God, but the Devill too. It is worth the observing, how the Devill once served them upon such a presuming as this, Acts 19. 13. and 16. But what say they for all this? Bold Bayard once dasht out the Witches braines. Never tell them; they have alwayes observed that Witches least hurt them, that worst use them; and they that are least affraid of them, still fare best by them. Oh! how the Devil dissembles a feare of those men whose Cases are most to bee feared? how hee spares them Temporally, that he may not spare them spiritually and eternally? what cares he for bewitching their Bodies, when hee has thus bewitched their better parts, their soules?

Thus having removed all false means; Though we here approve of no kind of exercising, much lesse admit it as an ordinary calling in the Church of Christ; yet we freely professe, that God hath not here left his church destitute of sufficient and lawfull Remedies, whether Preservative or Restorative. And these be; 1. A Conscionable care against sin, the old Witch of all. That did Effascinate our first Parents, and us in their loyns; but since hath directly bewitched us, both in our professions, Gal. 3. 1. as also in our Conversations, 1 Sam. 15. 23. That hath made us make a Covenant with Death, and an Agreement with Hell, Isa. 28. 15. That hath brought us to an Abnegation of the sacred Trinity; and to a corruption and profanation, both of Word and Sacraments. That makes us beleeve wee are Lords and Ladies of our own Wils; when wee are the only servile wretches, led Captive by Satan at his Will.

That rewards onely with meer delusions of momentary pleasures, to the hazard of eternall paines. More especially it behoves us to take heed of all such sinnes as (besides the Devill) more particularly expose us to the Witch. And they are, 1. Morose Cogitations; For they tempt God to give us over to visible temptations. 2. Dire Imprecations; for they want only Gods saying Amen unto them. 3. Tyrannous and oppressive Actions; for they cause the Lord to depart from us, and an evill spirit from the Lord to trouble us. 4. Hypocriticall professions; For if the uncleane spirit finde his house empty of all true graces, and swept only by an outward Restraint, of some more scandalous and notorious vices: and Garnished with simulated vertues, superfluous observations, affected garbes, and formall services: then hee taketh with himselfe seven other spirits, &c. Matth. 12. 44, 45. And it is to be noted how the Devill has always delighted to haunt & frequent Monasteries, Nunneries, and old Abbeys, places of so much hypocrisie. 5. Superstitious and profane communications, especially of Devills, Witches, and Witch-finders. We have some stories of such as by making these their Table-talke, have made themselves the more obnoxious to their infestations. It is strange to tell what superstitious opinions, affections, relations, are generallyrisen amongst us, since the Witch-finders came into the Countrey. And I pray God that these things doe not dispose & expose us to Witches, rather then help to ridde us of them.

2. Next to a care against sins; is an endeavour after graces. And those 1. Faith, for that makes every way strong to resist the Devill, 1 Pet. 5. 8, 9. 2. Purity of heart, for the unclean spirit findes no rest in dry places, Mat. 12. 43. And to let him find no rest in us, is the way not to be molested by him in any kind. 3. Prayer and fasting, for these are prevalent against the worst kind of them, Matth. 17. 21. 4. Confidence in Christs name and power, word and promises, Mark. 16. 17. 5. Frequent reading

and meditating upon the holy Scriptures, for ther's the sword of the Spirit, to pierce the head of the huge Leviathan: There's the voyce of the wise Charmer, to make the deafe Adder, and the olde Serpent burst in pieces. Search we there, & apply we the speciall promises & consolations for our particular Case, Gen. 3. 15. Ps. 91. 11, 12, 13. Joh. 16. 33. 1 Joh. 3. 8. Mar. 16. 17. Rom. 16. 20. 1 Cor. 10. 13. Jam. 4. 7. 1 Pet. 5. 9. But we must take heede of profaning Scripture names, phrases, and fragments; as Witches themselves do, in their most execrable witchcrafts. Or of setting apart certaine incompetent, and in-concerning verses for Charms, as the Papists do and teach. 6. The Prayers of the Church or Congregation, for they avayle exceedingly in any manner of Infirmity, Jam. 5. 14, 15. 7. Thanksgiving to God for his speciall providence; Blessing and praysing him for his own protection, & Angells administration. 8. A keeping us within our owne Callings, so shal the Devil find us, neither idle, nor ill occupied; so shall occasion be avoyded either for him to tempt us, or we him. 9. A just contempt of the Devill, and of all his praestigious. Arts and Instruments, Jer. 10. 2. as not to bee secure, so not to feare, for the Devill is a false spirit, & smiles in fayning a yieldance to a fond presumption: But hee's a proud one too, and therefore cannot be more vext and troubled then at a just & true Contempt.

X

Whether it be lawfull to consult with a Witch, upon any occasion?

Al consulting properly implies; as if one would now be informed by another, of what he would know, or Advised what he should doe: Either of which are very improperly sought for at a witches hand, that indeed knows neither truth, nor right, and in express opposition to whom God has been pleased to appoint for his a far better Counsellor in that Case, Esa. 8. 19. 20. Neneverthelese, how madly have superstitious and profane people alwayes runne upon their devices to be here advised. Gen. 41. 8. 1 Sam. 28. 7. 2 King. 1. 2. Dan. 2. 2. Albeit God hath utterly prohibited and condemned it, Levi. 19. 31. and 20. 6. Deu. 18. 14. And that the old Ecclesiasticall Censures have been the same against all such consultation, as against witchcraft it selfe. And that some Civill or Politique Laws have decreed Death to the Consultor equally as to the Witch. And that it hath been the Common observation of all People, that none have ever thriven after so tempting an Attempt. And that the same Iudgments of God are yet in force against al such as heretofore. 2. King. 1. 4. 1 Chron. 10. 13.

Upon these many Considerations I conclude, that althoug

one way is more damnable, yet there is danger in Consulting every kind of way. Whether out of Curiositie, or for Exploration sake, as wel as out of superstition.

1. If out of Curiosity onely to see and here, and tel what a witch or wizzard can say or doe. This is out of any mans calling or Commission, and so fals under a tempting of God.

2. If for Exploration sake, so as to Examine and discover the Witch. Herein (though the Authority may be granted. for safe and good) yet speciall heed is to be had, either of adjuring, or yet of alluring the Divell or the Witch. Forto adjurea Witch, if it be done by way of humane obtestation and Intreaty, then is it palpable consulting: or if it be done by way of divine Attestation (charging and challenging in the name of God) what else is it then, but that we call Exorcizing? And likewise to Allure the Witch to do any Act of Witchcraft, (through disguise, dissimulation, fayre words, promises, or any other pretext) yea although it be with intent to descry or make discovery, yet even this is to do evill that good may come thereof. And therefore the Witch of Endor justly exclaimes against the injustice and Treachery of such an Inticement, although it might have beene to such an intent, 1 Sam. 28. 9. 12. Now then this it is, to enquire here over familiarly may bee to allure: To charge over highly is to adjure: but only to interrogate Rationally and Legally, this is safely and sufficiently to explore.

3. But the damnable consulting of all is, if out of Superstition; to be informed of what is Future, Absent, Lost; or to bee holpen against any strange handling whatsoeever. For here is the same Faith that is in the Witches operation and confederacie; and (at least) a mediate assenting and joyning society with the Devill. And a yeelding or acknowledging the Devill to bee the Author of helpe; which standeth in the Name of the Lord our God alone. Oh! that people would bee perswaded of it; then should we not heare so many fond Objections, whereby they seek to

justifie themselves, and to evade all that can be said against them. But marke how little all they can say for themselves availes them: we will number their Objections, and set our Answer to them, not onely to refute, but instruct them.

1. I went for my owne satisfaction, and at my own hazzard, and what has any body to do with it? Yes, the Church has to doe with it, and censure it, as inconsistent with her communion, 2 Cor. 6. 15. The State hath to doe with it, and punish it, as enemy to the Society thereof. For the Diabolicall associating must needes be adversary to the Humane. Nay, and every private Christian hath to doe with it, to complaine of the grievous scandall thereof, and require satisfaction.

2. It was not a Witch that I went to, but a Wizzard, a Wise man, or a Wise woman, as they call them. All Witches are not of one kinde: and severall kindes are not of seveverall Natures: neither doth variety of degrees varie the kindes or natures. Things may be of the same brood or Litter, though unlike one another; and every one not so like the Damme.

3. It was neither Witch nor Wizzard, but a Jugling Impostor. But thou wentest as to a Witch indeed. The delusive event, excuses not the delusion of thy intention.

4. I went to none but a good Witch. Who ever cald a Witch good, but bad men? and if the Devil were called good, wouldst thou therefore goe to him?

5. I meant nobody hurt in it. A good meaning will not warrant the use of ill meanes.

6. It was not I that went, but my wife, childe, servant. Nomore was it Ahaziah, but his wife, 2 Kings 1. Aske but thy conscience, if thy heart went not along with them, either in the command or consent.

7. I medled with none of their witcheries, &c. Thy faith or perswasion to be satisfi'd and resolv'd in the Businesse thou went'st about, was enough to mingle thee with the Witch in

her confederacy. Nay, thou wast the very cause of that Act of Witchery that was now practised for thy sake, and upon thy occasion.

8. I saw nothing, I found nothing but good. All good is to bee suspected that comes from the Devill, who never did any thing like to good, but for the greater ill.

9. I was told nothing but Truth. The Devill is a Lyar of himselfe, and never told Truth, but to deceive. Some light Truth peradventure, and that either forcibly, or against his Will; or fortuitously and without his knowledge; or falsely to deceive thee in a greater Truth, and others with greater Lyes. Hee that looks to heare Truth from the Devill, may soon hear it to his sorrow, as did Sanl, 1 Sam. 28. 19.

10. I went but to see if I might bee inform'd or finde what I had lost. What was all that losse, to the losse of thy Credit and Conscience? Nay, not onely losse of peace within thy selfe, and of Reputation with wise men: But of Report with good men, & of favour with God. What if thou had'st not found? then was thy labour and hopes lost to all the rest. Say thou didd'st finde, it comming by the Devills meanes, comes with Gods Curse. Thus is it lost though found. Nay, and (in thy sense) shall be lost againe. For (besides that God blowes upon it) the Devill (since thou art so ready to seek after him) will be ready the second time to bereave thee either of that, or as much as that comes to, that so he may make thee seek to him againe. Thus shalt thou be continually the loser, and the Devill the Gainer: whereas hadd'st thou either despised thy losse, or despised this way of finding it, thy losse had not onely rested there; but thou hadst beene a great Gainer by Gods grace and blessing.

11. What would you have me doe? I could not endure to see the poore Thing so strangely handled, but seek out some remedy for it; and no body could tell what disease it was, all Physick would doe it no good, &c. Because ordinary meanes

failed, was God therefore to bee deserted, and his greatest enemy addrest unto? But that I am resolv'd to speak English only in this Epitome: I could further reply, out of an Ancient Fathers owne words to one that had procured a Charme to cure his Child, and objecting, What, would you have it perish? Yea, let it perish; better it perish then thou; it temporally, then thou eternally. What should I tell of Christians that have refused to touch, take up, or once remove a Witches Charm, Spell, Signe; no not for their owne present Cure? Nay, and of very Heathens that have derided and rejected all such remedies?

12. I did it onely in an humour, because I had a mind, or Fancy to know mine owne Fate or Fortune, &c. Because this is indeed the Fancy and Humour of too many: Let them hear what I say now unto them, in sundry considerations. 1. So did Saul, and heard his destiny to his utter despaire, 1 Sam. 28. 19, 20. 2. All future things are reserved in Gods owne knowledge and power; and therefore solely to be referred to him. 3. Who (of men or Angels) have been his Counsellors to be ordinarily acquainted with any such mysteries? 4. For a man to bee foreacquainted with his own Fortune; though it were expedient, yet is it not lawfull: And though it were lawfull, yet is it not expedient. For if good things be presaged to him, and they false; that makes him miserable in a frustrated hope: If bad things, and yet false, that makes him miserable in a needlesse feare: If bad things and true, they make a man miserable in his owne apprehension, before he is so in himselfe. If good things and true, yet the long Expectation both crucifies and takes off the edge of Delight in their Fruition. 5. When did ever any Diabolicall Predictions want their Ambiguities or Equivocation? For so fallaciously doth the Devill use to frame his Oracles, as that they may stand good with either event; to the end we may be either way deceived, and yet he neither way thought to deceive. 6. Is there any certainty of their fore telling

things future, that are ignorant of what is past or present? or how can they tell what shall betide another, that are not aware of what may befall themselves? 7. Have not the sager Heathens derided all Astronomicall, Genethliacall, Physiognomicall Presages and Predictions; and are they things to be believ'd by Christians? 8. He that will easily believe the Devill upon his Word, can hardly have any right faith of God in his Promises: For credulity to Satan, is to God-ward infidelity. 9. One that is here over anxiously, or curiously inquisitive, as he hath much of the Infidelity of an Atheist: so not a little of the Carnality of an Epicure. For 'tis a manifest Token he both loves, and likewise feares himselfe too much as touching the Body and present Being.

XI

WHAT PUNISHMENTS ARE WITCHES WORTHY OF; OR MAY JUSTLY BE INFLICTED ON THEM.

That Witches are to be punished is the Law and sentence of Nature, Reason, Policie and Religion. Nature sayes so, because they abuse her order: Reason says so, because they change her dictates for delusion: Policy sayes so, because they disturb her peace: and Religion sayes so, because they pervert her power. Hence have proceeded all those bitter invectives of Heathen & meer naturall men; all those solid irrefutations of Learned men & Philosophers; all those severe Edicts of Princes and Magistrates; and all those sharpe censures of the Church against them.

To pronounce sentence therefore in a word; a Witch, (a reall ranke Witch) is worthy of all poenalty that can either be inflicted or imagineth More then Temporal, Spirituall and Eternall punishment cannot be devised; and al these are here deserved.

1. Spirituall punishment, even the heavyest Anathema, or greatest Excommunication, Deut. 18. 10. Ezek. 12. 24. Mic. 5. 12. John 12. 31. 1 Cor. 10, 20. 2 Cor. 6. 14, 15, 16. And great reason that Witches should first be spiritually or Ecclesiastically

punished, 1. Because the sin of a Witch is (formally considered) a meere spirituall sin. 2. Witches primely abnegate and abjure the Churches Faith and fellowship: And therefore should first of all bee cast out of their Communion.

3. It is just Talion to deliver such up to Satan that have already given themselves unto him.

2. Temporall punishment, Exod. 22. 18. Levit. 20. 27. And the reasons are, 1. Because the Fact and Effects of witch-craft are Externall, and disturbing the Civill peace. 2. Witches in joyning Confoederacy with the Devill become profest Enemies to all true humane society, and therefore deserve to be cut off from it. 3. Their toleration is pernicious both to Church and State, not only in regard of their Maleficiating mischiefes, but also of Gods judgments, Isa. 47. 9. 12. Nahum 3. 4. 2 Kings 23. 26. Conferr'd with 2 King. 21. 6. 4. Because the longer Witches are suffered to live, the worse they are, not onely do more mischiefe to others, but grow more wicked within themselves. Humane mercy will never amend them; nor the Devil never forsake them til they fall under the Magistrates hand, and if ever they repent it is then, or not at all.

3. Eternal punishment, Rev. 21. 8. and 22. 15. And there's Reason for that too. 1. It is just that they who utterly deny God should be utterly denyed of him. 2. That they who give themselves to the Devill, and worship him; should goe to him, and receive their reward.

But the maine of the Case is touching Civill poenalty. And if you ask what particular punishment is to bee inflicted? The Scripture saith stoning, Levit. 20. 27. Authors in their Stories likewise store us with Lawes and Presidents of their hanging, heading, burning, drowning, fleaing off their skinnes, breaking upon the wheel, casting down headlong from steepe hills and Rockes, cutting theirh troats, pressing, racking, beating with stripes, braining with clubbs, banishment, imprisonmẽt, degradation, privation of office, forfeitur of estate, &c. Thus thought they no punishment enough for Witches. All which Inflictions, Witches (absolute witches) may be well worthy of. But God forbid they should be thus punished for Witches; that indeed are no Witches. For so Innocent blood may be brought upon a Land. Yet I speak not this, as if some who are Impostors only, or but coūfeit Witches (as Juglers, Gypsies, fortune-tellers, Figure-casters, Wizzards, Conjurers, Calculaters of Nativities, with false prophets and Prognosticators, that presume to presage what Changes shall be either in Church or State, should be unpunished. But that true and reall Witches should bee truly and really punished, to true and real intents. And that Magistrates and men in place, may wisely and justly preserve and discharge a good conscience, and do no otherwise (in this Case) then as Josiah did, 2 King. 23. 24. Where note, 1. His wisedome in discerning; They were spyed out in the Land: A word noting perspection, and circumspection; and that both of the mind and senses. Shewing how both the internall and externall powers of discerning should bee employed, and weighing both the Abstruse Mysterie; and more palpable materiall Circumstances thereof. 2. His Integrity or sincerity. That he might perform the words of the law, &c. Looking at nothing more then the honour of God, the justice of the Law, the Trueth of the Church, and the peace of the Common-wealth. But to take heed of doing (in such a Case) as Saul did, 1 Sam. 28. 3. who may well be deemed now to have done al smisterly. 1. Because if the Intention of his heart had been right to cut them off; then doubtlesse had it not been so soon disposed to consult with them. 2. It is surmized hee lookt onely at his owne private sufferance by such, 1 Sam. 16. 14. and not at the Law of GOD or publique good. 3. The Jewish Rabbines say that hee did it enviously. Because the Diviners also foretold of his Ejection from the Kingdome, and of DavidsElection therunto. And something is observable to such a purpose, in that Samuels death, and the Witches execution are mentioned both together. Noting hee forbare to execute his malice upon them while Samuel liv'd. Because Samuel (a Prophet of the Lord) had also foretold the same. 4. Some learned Protestants are of opinion that under pretext of Witches Saul now slew the Gibeonites, for which the judgment followed, 2 Sam. 21. 1. Neither indeed want we the storyed Examples of GODS Judgements upon those that defamed, prosecuted, and executed them for Witches, that indeed were none.

Wherefore I make bold to propose here these Cautionary Quaeries to bee considered, 1. Whether all kinds of Witches are to bee punished with one kind of punishmēt? And hereto I answer vulgarly at first hearing, God forbid. And doe confesse further, that I have read divers Laws cited for divers degrees of Mulcts & poenalties. Whereto I may adde also our owne Statute Law in that behalf wherein (in my poor judgment) severall kindes and measures of poenalties are well Enacted against several kinds and degrees of Witches. And I could wish with all my heart, that in the execution it were but so sctrictly observed, as in the Law it selfe is wisely provided.

2. Whether a Witch is to be punished capitally for the Pact or for the Fact of witchcraft? I know some (both Papists and Protestants) that are eager for denouncing upon the Pact alone, without any Fact done. And would have Witches cut off (as men kill Serpents) before they have once stung or poyson'd any. But (under correction of better judgments) I am bold also to pronounce my opinion. That although the meere Pact bee mortall before God: yet neither the Pact without the Fact; nor the Fact without the Pact, is to be Capitall before men. 1. Not the Pact without the Fact. For so it is not onely a meer spirituall sinne, a meer sinne of thought; but may be a meer Dreame or Delusion. Neither do I beleive there was ever in any

a reall pact, without a reall Fact. For the Devill does not now Confederate for nothing; nor will hee suffer his Associate to be idle. Neither is the Covenant, but for the Arts sake; nor the Art, but for the Practise. Neither yet can a Pact be well suspected, or prooved but by some kind of Fact. The Witch of Endor, 1 Sam. 28. was so Notoriously known to bee a Pacted Witch. that Sauls Servantscould tell him of her, at first asking, and of the Familiar Spirit shee had, vers. 7. yet does shee onely plead against Saul, for alluring her to the Fact, and so subjecting her to the penalty of the Law, ver. 9. which plainly declares that the Actor pleaded and the Guilty apprehended their Obnoxiousnes to the penalty of that Law from the FACT, and not from the Pact alone. 2. Not for the Fact, without the Pact. For then it is to bee conceived and Censured as the Effect of some other sinne or Crime, and not formally of Witchcraft. A parent (like as Witches use) curses his Child, and God sayes A men to it. Hereupon the Child is obsessed, or strangely handled (peradventur perishes, a thing of two common Example) But what? must the Parent hang for the Malefice? no; and why? Because here is onely the Factor Effect without the Pact.

3. Whether the Implicite Compact be lyable to the like poenalty as the Explicite? An Implicite Covenant is solely in the Faith and assent, now prodigious Effects may follow without any other Familiarity. And whether Familiarity so far forth as invisible Faith & Assent, be Felony, it is not in me to determine. Only I desire to be satisfyed what difference is between this, and the Faith and Assent in every deeply malitious sinne? For that likewise Implicitly makes a malignant Covenant with the Devill. Esa. 28. 15. Mee thinkes there should bee some Differences made betweene them; and that very Demonstratively. I have labored to Excogitate them, but finde it Difficult to set them so really Disparate and distinct as I would, in Affection, Intention Operation. For to me there appears in all something of the same

Corruption. And this very difficulty tells my Conscience what a wary discerning should here be for Censure and Poenalty. Neverthelesse I do not judg those, that shall proceed to judge them, upon a clearer distinguishing and discerning.

4. Whether one addicted to the speculative way onely ought to incurre the same poenalty with the operative Witches? I am not of those that contend for the lawfulnesse of Magical science. Because I cannot reach (in my judgement) to conceive, how it can be preserved (by such as wade too far into it) in the pure Naturalls: but must needs (what through Ignorance or Arroganee) bee polluted and deprav'd with some kind of delusions diabolicall. Notwithstanding doe I not reprove the knowledge of these things altogether. Lest I might reprove Moses and Daniel, Acts 7. 22. Daníel, 17. 20. Who knew them not to use or practise them; But to detect, and refute them: or knew them to the perfection of the understanding, not to the depravation of the Will. Yet doe I thinke those worthy to bee reprehended that shall affect, commend or promote this studie, (A studie as the most difficult, so the most uselesse) yea and to be censured too. But neverthelesse not like the Operative that have hereby wrought mischiefe or offence to the disturbance of peace and truth, in the Church and State. Unlesse laying aside all Scrutiny and Contemplation as touching the Mirables of Nature, their Speculation be of Diabolicall Magicke only: in Contemplating and musing of (I cannot tell what) Compact, Conventicles, Rites, Sacrifices, Invocations, Conjuratiõs, Charms, Spells, Characters, Figures, Circles, Barbarismes of words, Prodigies of Fact, &c. Admiring, adoring, boasting, commending, teaching, &c. These (as Masters and Professors in witchcrafts) I thinke worthy most punishment of all.

5. Whether a Passive witch be to be punished by the Law as well as an Active? How extreame were it therfore to suffer from men; because they suffer from the Devil? Can his excruciation

be a sufficient Cause for our Execution? I conceive the meerly passive therefore are here to be exempted. Because though the Devil works by them, yet it is without them, yea & oft times against them. Neverthelesse the mixtly passive, may be distinguished from those who are lesse to be pitied or spared because though they may now be somwhat passive, and the Devill (as it were) forcing them to malefice or mischiefe; yet they first were Active, and freely gave their consent so to do.

6. Whether a Witches own Confession bee sufficient to hang her? I cannot see (in the maine) but a Witch may bee condemned out of her owne mouth as well as any other Malefactor. For her owne mouth can speake, her owne guilt best, and may not amisse be taken for a right discovery of her own Conscience. Nor doth her Sexe any whit invalidher own testimonie against her self. Nevertheless it would be wel considered whether she was forced to it, terrified, allured, or otherwise deluded. And withall, if in her owne mind and perfect senses; If not out of some Melancholy humour or discontentment working to say any thing through tediousnesse of life; If her Recollection or recantation may not stand with more probability if they be not meer impossibilities whereof not a Circumstance tending to such a matter, can bee made to appear. But it matters not much, though shee talke of never so many monstrous or ridiculous Delusions or absurdities, (for the Devills Actions are now to be admitted for no lesse) if so be some Reality of depraved Affections, Intentions, or Effects may be observed therein.

7 Whether a Jury may with a safe Conscience give up their Verdict in finding such or such an one for a witch? Doubtles it may be done. For whatsoever sinne or Crime is punishable before men, is also Convincible by men. Otherwise all Lawes against them were to no Effect. For the Law is not to be Executed before the Sentence bee pronounced; nor ought that to be before Conviction. Neither is it requisite that so palpable

Evidence for Conviction should here come in, as in other more sensible matters. It is enough if there be but so much Circumstantiall proofe or evidence; as the Substance, matter, and Nature of such an Abstruse mystery of Iniquitie will well admit. But withall I could wish that these Twelve good men and True, were not Impannelled of ordinary Country People: but of the most Eminent Physitians, Lawyers and Divines, that a Country could afford.

8 What if there be no such maine Evidence against Witches; Are they therefore to be Tolerated or to Escape? Some are of opinion that a strong Presumption is enough to cut them off: but that were a strōg Presumption indeed; others, that it is good to hang thē out of the way however for terror and Examples sake: A terrible thing indeed, to make them Examples in the Punishment that are not yet fully found to be Examples in the offence. Others would have it done and it be but for their repentance and Conversion. Because (say they) Witches will never thinke of Repenting till they come to the Gallowes. Were it so, it were then happy for the Wretches; But say it were so, Gods mercy excuses not mans Injustice, but aggravates it. In my mind therefore this is safest, and satisfactory; where God hath denyed man full evidence, it is not for mans Iustice to fall to Execution of vengeance: Nor is that to be called Tolleration where Conviction is wanting. This is plain in more sensible Cases (as of Murther, Theft &c.) where the Law proceeds not (though upō never so strong Presumptions) for want of Plenary and particular Evidence; and why not here sith it is a Matter more occult? And if it remaynes so occult, as not to come within a Legal conviction; it is a signe God hath reserved such for his owne Iustice and Vengeance which all their devillish Darknesse shall not be able to elude, Malac. 3. 5. Hee will draw neare to their Iudgment though they think themselves never so far from mans. He will be a swift Witnesse against them, when

mans is either slow or insufficient.

XII

WHETHER A WITCH MAY REPENT, AND SO BE SAVED?

I know the Churches of old have been so Charitable, as to suppose their Conversion: and to that purpose, have (in severall Cases) proposed their penance. And I read in Story of the Notable Repentance of certaine Pope Witches; with the miraculous signes of their salvation. And have heard the Tradition, how the Devill has been forc't to cast up and Cancell some such pacting Indentures, though written with the Partyes owne Blood. I will conceive withall, that Witches have as great Cause as may be to recant them of their bargaine, and Labour to returne. Because they have made a Covenant with one, that (on his part) never intended to performe the least Tittle promised, otherwise then praestigiously. They serve a hard Master, that hates them according to an irreconcileable Enmity, Gen. 3. 15. notwithstanding all the pretended Familiarity: and not onely so, but renders them hatefull both to God, & Men. That infests their habitation night, & day; torments them sleeping and waking; terrifies them with gastly sights, & hideous sounds; makes them familiar to the most loathsome Creatures, wherein are least footesteps of the Creator to be perceived. Haunts them continually, to be still imploying their Imps about one Mischiefe or another: and will not suffer (would a Witch be so good) to remove the evill done to any one, but by transferring it upon some other; or else threatens to inflict it upon themselves. Keeps them alwayes poore, leane, naked, diseased, discontented; and deludes them utterly in their most Imaginary pleasures and Contentments. If they chance to steale any thing after a prodigious manner, he straightwayes as praestigiously conveys it from them againe; or so infects it that it is nothing usefull to them. And after once wholly his seekes to betray them to Temporall Justice, that so he may the sooner get them into his infernall Possession; and this he is the more eager upon, lest peradventure having wearyed themselves in this way of wickednes it might come into their minds to repent them at length. And thus we have the Devill also fearing their repentance; and by that it should seeme there is some hopes of them. There would be more hope if wee could heare God promising and promoving it. But God hath universally declared himselfe for their damnation. Malac. 3. 5. Revel. 21. 8. and 22. 15. And it is safest alwayes to judge after his Sentence. Wherefore though witches may have some slender thoughts and wishes for salvation, as had Balaam, Numb. 24. 10. Yet I cannot but thinke it a rare thing still for Magitians to come and worship Christ. Mat. 2. 1, 2.

As to the Case therefore; to say that of Witches, Some may Convert and be saved; some cannot Convert, but shall bee Damned. This were to leave the Case as Indefinite, as I found it. For lesse then so cannot be determined concerning the least of sins. Give me leave therefore to declare the Judgement of my Conscience both somewhat more determinately and distinctly. viz. That the Arted Passive and simply Deluded Witch may repent and be saved: But the solemnly Pacted, malitiously Active, and utterly Apostate Witch neither can, nor will, nor shall. The Arted Witches, Act. 19. 13 Converted and so were saved. For the word of God prevailed to that Purpose. vers. 20. Yea they beleved and shewed their Deeds. vers. 18. But Simon Magus though heeused the meanes of Salvation (hee beleeved, wondred and was Baptized, Act. 8. 13.) Yet neither had hee part nor lot in the matter of Sanctification or Salvation, ver. 21. yea, though the Apostle puts a peradventure upon his Repentance, Prayer, Remission; yet is hee peremptory upon his Reprobation, vers. 22. 23. And all is because of the Diabolicall and Indissoluble Pact the Bond of Iniquity. So the Damsell, Act. 16. 16. 17. 18. A meerly passive Witch (whose Divination or Soothsaying was forced thorow a Daemoniacal Possession) was saved no doubt. Of which her opportune Occursion, her Confession, her Application of it, her perseverance, with Satans Ejection out of her, are sufficient Testimonies. But I cannot say so much of Jezabel and the witch of Endor, who were malicious active witches. Manasseh likewise (though some think hee was no Witch himselfe, but only a Consulter, a Favourer and a promoter of them) yet (led by the many notable Expressions, 2 Chr. 39. 6.) I rather conceive he was a very Witch. Neverthelesse it is said he sought the Lord, and prayed, and the Lord was entreated of him, vers. 12. 13. But he was no Apostate Witch. For it is not spoken of him til after his Conversion. He then knew that the Lord he was God, v. 13. But Simon Magus and Elymas the Sorcerer (two Apostate witches) who would have hired the power of the holy Spirit for money, who maliciously sought to pervert the faith & truth of Christ. These therefore the Apostles (Peter and Paul) denounce expresly for damned Reprobates, Act. 8. 23. and 13. 8, 9, 10.

To conclude, when I shal be instructed, of any one particular and specifique sin, so neare to the sinne against the holy Ghost as this of Witchcraft: Or that there is any other blasphemy more imputing the works of the Devill to God, or the workes of God to the Devill: or such an Anti-christian Misterie of Iniquity with lying wonders, and strong delusions, 2 Thess. 2. Or such a giving heed to seducing spirits and doctrines of Devills, 1 Tim. 4. Or such a treading under foot the Son of God, counting the Blood of the Covenant a vaine thing, and doing despight unto the Spirit of grace, Heb. 10. Or in very deed such a sin unto death, 1 John 5. I say, when I shall be instructed that the sin of Witchcraft is not all this: Or if there bee any other specifique particular sinne so like to all this, as is the sinne of Witchcraft: Or to which both the Scripture phrases and properties that Divines make of the sinne against the Holy Ghost, may bee more aptly and fully apply'd, then shall I bee convicted in Conscience to bee more remisse in my Judgement against the Pacted-Active-Apostate Witch.

FINIS.

THE
Discovery of Witches:

IN

Answer to severall QUERIES,

LATELY

Delivered to the Judges of Assize for the County of NORFOLK.

And now published

By MATTHEVV HOPKINS, Witch-finder.

FOR

The Benefit of the whole KINGDOME.

EXOD. 22. 18.

Thou shalt not suffer a witch to live.

LONDON,
Printed for *R. Royston*, at the Angell in Ivie Lane.
M. DC. XLVII.

Matthew Hopkins Witch Finder Generall
My Imps names are
Holt.
1 Ilemauzar
2 Pyewackett
Jarmara
3 Pecke in the Crowne
4 Griezzell Greedigutt
Sacke & Sugar
Newes
Vinegar tom

THE DISCOVERY OF WITCHES

IN Answer to severall QUERIES, LATELY Delivered to the Judges of Assize for the County of NORFOLK

And now published

by MATTHEW HOPKINS, Witch-finder.

FOR the Benefit of the whole KINGDOME

EXOD. 22.18.

Thou shalt not suffer a witch to live.

LONDON
Printed for R. Royston, at the Angell in Ivie Lane.
M.DC.XLVII.
(1647)

CERTAINE QUERIES ANSWERED, WHICH HAVE BEEN AND ARE LIKELY TO BE OBJECTED AGAINST MATTHEW HOPKINS, IN HIS WAY OF FINDING OUT WITCHES.

Querie 1.
That he must needs be the greatest Witch, Sorcerer, and Wizzard himselfe, else he could not doe it.

Answ.
If Satan's kingdome be divided against it selfe, how shall it stand?

Querie 2.
If he never went so farre as is before mentioned, yet for certaine he met with the Devill, and cheated him of his Booke, wherein were written all the Witches names in England, and if he looks on any Witch, he can tell by her countenance what she is; so by this, his helpe is from the Devill.

Answ.
If he had been too hard for the devill and got his book, it had been to his great commendation, and no disgrace at all: and for judgement in Phisiognomie, he hath no more then any man else whatsoever.

Quer. 3.
From whence then proceeded this his skill? was it from his profound learning, or from much reading of learned Authors concerning that subject?

Answ.
From neither of both, but from experience, which though it be meanly esteemed of, yet the surest and safest way to judge by.

Quer. 4.
I pray where was this experience gained? and why gained by him and not by others?

Answ.
The Discoverer never travelled far for it, but in March 1644 he had some seven or eight of that horrible sect of Witches living in the Towne where he lived, a Towne in Essex called Maningtree , with divers other adjacent Witches of other towns, who every six weeks in the night (being alwayes on the Friday night) had their meeting close by his house and had their severall solemne sacrifices there offered to the Devill, one of which this discoverer heard speaking to her Imps one night, and bid them goe to another Witch, who was thereupon apprehended, and searched, by women who had for many yeares knowne the Devills marks, and found to have three teats about her, which honest women have not: so upon command from the Justice they were to keep her from sleep two or three nights, expecting in that time to see her familiars, which the fourth night she called in by their severall names, and told them what shapes, a quarter of an houre before they came in, there being ten of us in the roome, the first she called was:

1. Holt, who came in like a white kitling.

2. Jarmara, who came in like a fat Spaniel without any legs at all, she said she kept him fat, for she clapt her hand on her belly and said he suckt good blood from her body.

3. Vinegar Tom, who was like a long-legg'd Greyhound, with an head like an Oxe, with a long taile and broad eyes, who when this discoverer spoke to, and bade him goe to the place provided for him and his Angels, immediately transformed himselfe into the shape of a child of foure yeeres old without a head, and gave halfe a dozen turnes about the house, and vanished at the doore.

4. Sack and Sugar, like a black Rabbet.

5. Newes, like a Polcat.

All these vanished away in a little time. Immediately after this Witch confessed severall other Witches, from whom she had her Imps, and named to divers women where their marks were, the number of their Marks, and Imps, and Imps names, as Elemanzer, Pyewacket, Peckin the Crown, Grizzel, Greedigut,&c. which no mortall could invent; and upon their searches the same Markes were found, the same number, and in the same place, and the like confessions from them of the same Imps, (though they knew not that we were told before) and so peached one another thereabouts that joyned together in the like damnable practise that in our Hundred in Essex , 29 were condemned at once, 4 brought 25 Miles to be hanged, where this Discoverer lives, for sending the Devill like a Beare to kill him in his garden, so by seeing diverse of the mens Papps, and trying wayes with hundreds of them, he gained this experience, and for ought he knowes any man else may find them as well as he and his company, if they had the same skill and experience.

Quer. 5.
Many poore People are condemned for having a Pap, or Teat about them, whereas many People (especially antient People) are, and have been a long time troubled with naturall wretts on severall parts of their bodies and other naturall excressencies, as Hemerodes, Piles, Childbearing, &c. and these shall be judged only by one man alone and a woman, and so accused or acquitted.

Answ.
The parties so judging can justifie their skill to any, and shew good reasons why such markes are not meerly naturall, neither that they can happen by any such naturall cause as is before expressed, and for further answer for their private judgements alone, it is most false and untrue, for never was any man tryed by search of his body, but commonly a dozen of the ablest men in the parish or else where, were present, and most commonly as many ancient skilfull matrons and midwives present when the women are tryed, which marks not only he, and his company attest to be very suspitious, but all beholders, the skilfulest of them, doe not approve of them, but likewise assent that such tokens cannot in their judgements proceed from any the above mentioned Causes.

Quer. 6.
It is a thing impossible for any or woman to judge rightly on such marks, they are so neare to naturall excressencies and they that finde them, durst not presently give Oath they were drawne by evil spirits, till they have used unlawfull courses of torture to make them say any thing for ease and quiet, as who would not do? but I would know the reasons he speakes of, how, and whereby to discover the one from the other, and so be satisfied in that.

Answ.
The reasons in breefe are three, which for the present he judgeth to differ from naturall marks which are:

1. He judgeth by the unusualnes of the place where he findeth the teats in or on their bodies being farre distant from any usuall place, from whence such naturall markes proceed, as if a witch plead the markes found are Emerods, if I finde them on the bottome of the back-bone, shall I assent with him, knowing they are not neere that veine, and so others by child-bearing, when it may be they are in the contrary part?

2. They are most commonly insensible, and feele neither pin, needle, aule, &c. thrust through them.

3. The often variations and mutations of these marks into severall formes, confirmes the matter; as if a Witch hear a month or two before that the Witch- finder (as they call him) is comming they will, and have put out their Imps to others to suckle them, even to their owne young and tender children; these upon search are found to have dry skinnes and filmes only, and be close to the flesh, keepe her 24 houres with a diligent eye, that none of her Spirits come in any visible shape to suck her; the women have seen the next day after her Teats extended out to their former filling length, full of corruption ready to burst, and leaving her alone then one quarter of an houre, and let the women go up againe and shee will have them drawn by her Imps close againe: Probatum est. Now for answer to their tortures in its due place.

Quer. 7.
How can it possibly be that the Devill bring a spirit, and wants no nutriment or sustentation, should desire to suck any

blood? and indeed as he is a spirit he cannot draw any such excressences, having neither flesh nor bone, nor can be felt, &c.

Ans.
He seekes not their bloud, as if he could not subsist without that nourishment, but he often repairs to them, and gets it, the more to aggravate the Witches damnation, and to put her in mind of her Covenant; and as he is a Spirit and Prince of the ayre, he appeares to them in any shape whatsoever, which shape is occasioned by him through joyning of condensed thickned aire together, and many times doth assume shapes of many creatures; but to create any thing he cannot do it, it is only proper to God: But in this case of drawing out of these Teats, he doth really enter into the body, reall, corporeall, substantiall creature, and forceth that Creature (he working in it) to his desired ends, and useth the organs of that body to speake withall to make his compact up with the Witches, be the creature Cat, Rat, Mouse, &c.

Quer. 8.
When these Paps are fully discovered, yet that will not serve sufficiently to convict them, but they must be tortured and kept from sleep two or three nights, to distract them, and make them say any thing; which is a way to tame a wilde Colt, or Hawke, &c.

Ans.
In the infancy of this discovery it was not only thought fitting, but enjoyned in Essex and Suffolke by the Magistrates, with this intention only, because they being kept awake would be more the active to cal their imps in open view the sooner to their helpe, which oftentimes have so happened; and never or seldome did any Witch ever complaine in the time of their

keeping for want of rest, but after they had beat their heads together in the Goale; and after this use was not allowed of by the judges and other Magistrates, it was never since used, which is a yeare and a halfe since, neither were any kept from sleep by any order or direction since; but peradventure their own stubborne wills did not let them sleep, though tendered and offered to them.

Quer. 9.
Beside that unreasonable watching, they were extraordinarily walked, till their feet were blistered, and so forced through that cruelty to confesse, &c.

Ans.
It was in the same beginning of this discovery, and the meaning of walking of them at the highest extent of cruelty, was only they to walke about themselves the night they were watched, only to keepe them waking: and the reason was this, when they did lye or sit in a chaire, if they did offer to couch downe, then the watchers were only to desire them to sit up and walke about, for indeed when they be suffered so to couch, immediately comes their Familiars into the room and scareth the watchers, and heartneth on the Witch, though contrary to the true meaning of the same instructions, diverse have been by rusticall People, (they hearing them confess to be Witches) mis-used, spoiled, and abused, diverse whereof have suffered for the same, but could never be proved against this Discoverer to have a hand in it, or consent to it; and hath likewise been un-used by him and others, ever since the time they were kept from sleepe.

Quer. 10.
But there hath been an abominable, inhumane, and unmercifull tryall of these poore creatures, by tying them, and heaving them

into the water; a tryall not allowable by Law or conscience, and I would faine know the reasons for that.

Ans.
It is not denyed but many were so served as had Papps, and floated, others that had none were tryed with them and sunk, but marke the reasons.

For first the Divels policie is great, in perswading many to come of their own accord to be tryed, perswading them their marks are so close they shall not be found out, so as diverse have come 10 or 12 Miles to be searched of their own accord, and hanged for their labour, (as one Meggs, a Baker, did, who lived within 7 Miles of Norwich, and was hanged at Norwich Assizes for witchcraft) then when they find that the Devil tells them false they reflect on him, and he (as 40. have confessed) adviseth them to be sworne, and tels them they shall sinke and be cleared that way, then when they be tryed that way and floate, they see the Devill deceives them againe, and have so laid open his treacheries.

2. It was never brought in against any of them at their tryals as any evidence.

3. King James in his Demonology saith, it is a certaine rule, for (saith he) Witches deny their baptisme when they Covenant with the Devill, water being the sole element thereof, and therefore saith he, when they be heaved into the water, the water refuseth to receive them into her bosome, (they being such Miscreants to deny their baptisme) and suffers them to float, as the Froath on the Sea, which the water will not recieve, but casts it up and downe till it comes to the earthy element the shore, and there leaves it to consume.

4. Observe these generation of Witches, if they be at any time abused by being called Whore, Theefe, &c, by any where they live, they are the readiest to cry and wring their hands, and shed tears in abundance & run with full and right sorrowfull acclamations to some Justice of the Peace, and with many teares make their complaints: but now behold their stupidity; nature or the elements reflection from them, when they are accused for this horrible and damnable sin of Witchcraft, they never alter or change their countenances nor let one Teare fall. This by the way, swimming (by able Divines whom I reverence) is condemned for no way, and therefore of late hath, and for ever shall be left.

Quer. 11.

Oh! but if this torturing Witch-catcher can by all or any of these meanes wring out a word or two of confession from any of these stupified, ignorant, unitelligible, poore silly creatures, (though none heare it but himselfe) he will adde and put her in feare to confesse telling her, else she shall be hanged; but if she doe, he will set her at liberty, and so put a word into her mouth, and make such a silly creature confesse she knowes not what.

Answ.

He is of a better conscience, and for your better understanding of him, he doth thus uncase himselfe to all, add declares what confessions (though made by a Witch against her selfe) he allowes not of, and doth altogether account of no validity, or worthy of credence to be given to it, and ever did so account it, and ever likewise shall.

1. He utterly denyes that confession of a Witch to be of any validity, when it is drawn from her by any torture or violence whatsoever; although after watching, walking, or swimming,

diverse have suffered, yet peradventure Magistrates with much care and diligence did solely and fully examine them after sleepe, and consideration sufficient.

2. He utterly denyes that confession of a Witch, which is drawn from her by flattery, viz. if you will confess you shall go home, you shall not go to the Goale, nor be hanged, &c.

3. He utterly denyes that confession of a Witch, when she confesseth any improbability, impossibility, as flying in the ayre, riding on a broom, &c.

4. He utterly denyes a confession of a Witch, when it is interrogated to her, and words put into her mouth, to be of any force or effect: as to say to a silly (yet Witch wicked enough) you have foure Imps have you not? She answers affirmatively, Yes: Did they not suck you? Yes, saith she: Are not their names so, and so? Yes, saith shee; Did not you send such an Impe to kill my child? Yes saith she, this being all her confession after this manner, it is by him accompted nothing, and he earnestly doth desire that all Magistrates and Jurors would a little more then ever they did examine witnesses about the interrogated confessions.

Quer. 12.
If all those confessions be denyed, I wonder what he will make confession, for sure it is, all these wayes have been used and took for good confessions, and many have suffered for them, and I know not what, he will then make confession.

Answ.
Yes, in brief he will declare what confession of a Witch is of validity and force in his judgement, to hang a Witch: when a

Witch is first found with teats, then sequestred from her house, which is onely to keep her old associates from her, and so by good counsell brought into a sad condition, by understanding of the horribleness of her sin, and the judgements threatned against her; and knowing the Devils malice and subtile circumventions, is brought to remorse and sorrow for complying with Satan so long, and disobeying Gods sacred Commands, doth then desire to unfold her mind with much bitterness, and then without any of the before-mentioned hard usages or questions put to her, doth of her owne accord declare what was the occasion of the Devils appearing to her, whether ignorance, pride, anger, malice, &c. was predominant over her, she doth then declare what speech they had, what likeness he was in, what voice be had, what familiars he sent her, what number of spirits, what names they had, what shape they were in, what imployment she set them about to severall persons in severall places, (unknowne to the hearers) all which mischiefes being proved to be done, at the same time she confessed to the same parties for the same cause, and all effected, is testimony enough again her for all her denyall.

Quest. 13.
How can any possibly beleeve that the Devill and the Witch joyning together, should have such power, as the Witches confesse to kill such such a man, child, horse, cow, the like; if we beleeve they can doe what they will, then we derogate from Gods power, who for certaine limits the Devill and the Witch; and I cannot beleeve they have any power at all.

Answ.
God suffers the Devill many times to doe much hurt, and the devill doth play many times the deluder and impostor with these Witches, in perswading them that they are the cause of such

and such a murder wrought by him with their consents, when and indeed neither he nor they had any hand in it, as thus: We must needs argue, he is of a long standing, above 6000. yeers, then he must needs be the best Scholar in all knowledges of arts and tongues, & so have the best skill in Physicke, judgment in Physiognomie, and knowledge of what disease is reigning or predominant in this or that mans body, (and so for cattell too) by reason of his long experience. This subtile tempter knowing such a man lyable to some sudden disease, (as by experience I have found) as Plurisie, Imposthume, &c. he resorts to divers Witches; if they know the man, and seek to make a difference between the Witches and the party, it may be by telling them he hath threatned to have them very shortly searched, and so hanged for Witches, then they all consult with Satan to save themselves, and Satan stands ready prepared, with a What will you have me doe for you, my deare and nearest children, covenanted and compacted with me in my hellish league, and sealed with your blood, my delicate firebrand- darlings.

[Sidenote: The Divells speech to the Witches.]

Oh thou (say they) that at the first didst promise to save us thy servants from any of out deadly enemies discovery, and didst promise to avenge and flay all those, we pleased, that did offend us; Murther that wretch suddenly who threatens the down- fall of your loyall subjects. He then promiseth to effect it. Next newes is heard the partie is dead, he comes to the witch, and gets a world of reverence, credence and respect for his power and activeness, when and indeed the disease kills the party, not the Witch, nor the Devill, (onely the Devill knew that such a disease was predominant) and the witch aggravates her damnation by her familiarity and consent to the Devill, and so comes likewise in compass of the Lawes. This is Satans usuall impostring and deluding, but not his constant course of proceeding, for he and the witch doe mischiefe too much. But I would that Magistrates and Jurats would a little examine witnesses when they heare witches confess such and such a murder, whether the party had not long time before, or at the time when the witch grew suspected, some disease or other predominant, which might cause that issue or effect of death.

Quer. 14.
All that the witch-finder doth is to fleece the country of their money, and therefore rides and goes to townes to have imployment, and promiseth them
faire promises, and it may be doth nothing for it, and possesseth many men that they have so many wizzards and so many witches in their towne, and so hartens them on to entertaine him.

Ans.
You doe him a great deale of wrong in every of these particulars. For, first:

1. He never went to any towne or place, but they rode, writ, or sent often for him, and were (for ought he knew) glad of him.

2. He is a man that doth disclaime that ever he detected a witch, or said, Thou art a witch; only after her tryall by search, and their owne confessions, he as others may judge.

3. Lastly, judge how he fleeceth the Country, and inriches himselfe, by considering the vast summe he takes of every towne, he demands but 20s. a town, & doth sometimes ride 20 miles for that, & hath no more for all his charges thither and back again (& it may be stayes a weeke there) and finde

there 3 or 4 witches, or if it be but one, cheap enough, and this is the great summe he takes to maintaine his Companie with 3 horses.

Judicet ullus.

Printed in Great Britain
by Amazon

10767716R00150